BIBLE STORIES YOU NEVER HEARD BEFORE

BIBLE STORIES
YOU NEVER HEARD BEFORE

William R. Phillippe

Wm CAXTON LTD
Evanston, Illinois
Sister Bay, Wisconsin

Printed in the United States of America

10   9   8   7   6   5   4   3   2   1

Published by Wm Caxton Ltd, Box 709, Sister Bay, WI 54234

Library of Congress Cataloging-in-Publication Data

Phillippe, William R., 1930-
    Bible stories you never heard before.

    1. Bible. O.T.--Sermons. 2. Sermons, American.
3. Bible--History of Biblical events. I. Title.
BS1151.5.P47   1988   220.9'505   88-11830

ISBN 0-940473-06-2 (original paperback)

This book is dedicated to the kind and helpful members of congregations who have heard me preach for over three decades. Preaching, like many other skills, is developed by practice. As I have always had sympathy for those who have lived with a budding trumpeter, so I have great compassion for those who have had patience with me, especially in those early years.

Special appreciation goes to Linda and Roger Anderson whose support and encouragement led directly to this publication.

CONTENTS

PREFACE

Many adults, especially those over forty-five years of age, have heard the stories from the Old and New Testaments. But, these stories are generally told in a very literal way to prove some specific theological point or to express the position of a particular denomination or group of Christians. They are often told with a singular lack of humor and vitality, and they are almost always followed by some pietistic little moralism. Seldom did we learn as children the real reason why a story was included in the literature of our faith. Another problem is that the stories were seldom told in a way that gave the hearer any idea either of the context of the story itself or of the lives of the people involved. Most adults have forgotten the details of the stories, yet they are some of the best examples of storytelling available.

My objective here is to retell the stories in modern language, remaining true to the biblical base, but pointing out the context of the stories and the reasons why they are included in the history of our mothers and fathers in the faith.

Except for chapter 1, each of these chapters originated as a sermon. I have altered them somewhat for presentation here, but I am conscious that a sermon is a form of communication quite different from the written word. Sermons are intended to be heard, not read; they are meant to be experienced by a gathered people rather than by single individuals.

Many people ask me, after I have preached, how long it took to write a sermon. My answer is that it has taken something like thirty-three years. My sermons draw upon the accumulated knowledge and experience of all years of study and ministry, actually beginning at the time of a persons first consciousness.

Some of the sermons in this book were first preached (though in a far different form I must admit) in my first parish in King of Prussia, Pennsylvania. From the time I first committed them to writing they have swirled in my mind, and I have discovered that each time I preach them, I alter them significantly. I need also admit that because of this process some of them may well contain ideas and even phrasing from sources that I have not identified. I would dearly love to acknowledge such sources, but I cannot; they have entered my mind over the years and have become part of my attempt to interpret the Bible. I ask forgiveness for such borrowing, and at the same time I freely offer to others the use of thoughts and themes that I have developed over my years in the pastoral ministry of the Church.

William R. Phillippe
Summer 1988

Chapter One

AN OVERVIEW
OF OLD AND NEW TESTAMENT HISTORY
(OR, 1725 B.C. AND ALL THAT)

The first fairly well defined historic event of the Judaic/Christian faith history is set forth in *Genesis*, Chapter 12. All that goes before it is definitely prehistory, stories told around campfires to entertain and instruct both adults and children concerning some of the nagging questions of life. In the first eleven chapters of Genesis there are magnificently told stories of creation (there are two diametrically opposed versions in Chapters 1 and 2, but, hey, who was around to see it, much less verify the order of creation); of the two brothers Cain and Abel and their problems in getting along with each other; of the flood, which is God's attempt to begin all over again since things were not going well; and of the tower of Babel, another indication that the original intent of God that we stay in relationship both with the creator and with each other was irreparably messed up.

But with Chapter 12 we have a new beginning. The text is lean:

> Yahweh said to Abram, "Leave your country,
> your family and your father's house, for the land
> I will show you. I will make you a great nation;
> I will bless you and make your name so famous
> that it will be used as a blessing. . . ." [1]

---

[1] *Genesis* 12:1-2.

So our history begins with this event and quite an event it turned out to be. Abram, later called Abraham, took his wife, Sarah and his nephew Lot and all their combined "extended family" as well as their possessions, and walked about 1,000 miles around the Fertile Crescent to a land we now call Israel and Jordan.

The journey began from a city called Ur, near the Persian Gulf, and followed the grassland northwestward in a gentle arc that went around the north end of the high, dry Syrian and Arabian deserts. The procession may well have looked like a Barnum and Baily Circus parade for there could have been some 600 people and animals. Animals of all sorts came along, since they had to take their groceries with them. It would have been a slow-moving parade, for there had to be time for grazing, watering, and setting up and tearing down the camp.

The date of his event, as close as we can come, was around 1725 B.C. This date is established by references to other peoples that Abraham encounters on his journey and to place names in the account, and by discoveries of modern archaeologists.

Archaeological discoveries indicate that Abraham started his journey at a time when a group of persons called Amorites poured out of the desert to take control of the land between the Tigris and Euphrates rivers and then expanded up and around the Fertile Crescent and down into Palestine almost as far as Egypt. The best known king of this crowd was Hammurabi.

To put this into historical perspective, by this time the first pyramids in Egypt were already about 1,000 years old and the Chinese were well along the road of civilization.

So, in about 1725 B.C., Abraham and Sarah took the journey from Ur of the Chaldees, where the River Euphrates once joined the Persian Gulf, to the city of Haran near the headwaters of the Euphrates and then southward into Canaan.

Canaan was not a vacant lot. There were already people there, though it was probably thinly settled. Abraham is called a sojourner, significantly enough, not a settler at this point. He moves from place to place for many years in the manner of a nomad as does his son Isaac and grandson Jacob. The stories in Genesis of the families of Isaac and

Rebekah and of Jacob and his wives Rachael and Leah indicate that they had no great investment in that particular land.

The whole area of the Middle East gives the impression, from the perspective of this distance in time, of a seething cauldron of various tribes. From time to time they spill out of the inner deserts or high mountains and wrest control of the lower land and trade routes from others. I have already mentioned that Abraham's leaving may well have been part of the Amorite incursion, and now another large movement of people plays a significant role in our faith history.

A group known as the Hyksos, made up of a variety of ethnic backgrounds swept across the Middle East. Following the Fertile Crescent, they invaded, captured and controlled using a new war weapon, the chariot. They came south through Canaan and finally conquered Egypt, setting up a capital at Memphis. For over 150 years they dominated Egyptian history. Being a diverse people to begin with, they were quite charitable to other tribes of people who were driven to fertile Egypt by famine, including Jacob and his people.

One of Jacob and Rachael's sons, Joseph, was sold into slavery by his brothers and taken to Egypt. Joseph, who was quite bright, found his way into the service of the Hyksos kings (a not at all unusual practice) and rose quickly in the ranks. Remember that these were early days of invasion and control; someone like Joseph, a Semite like the Hyksos, would find this a fine time to get in and make it. He obviously did, eventually becoming chancellor, no less!

Soon afterward a severe famine occurred in Canaan, and Jacob took his whole tribe to Egypt. Under Joseph's guidance and protection they settled down in the rich delta land and became quite prosperous over the next several centuries.

But kings, dynasties and administrations rise, have their day, and fall, and so it was with the mighty Hyksos. The book of Exodus puts it quite succinctly:

> Then there came to power in Egypt a new king
> who knew nothing of Joseph. "Look," he said to
> his subjects "these people, the sons of Israel,
> have become so numerous and strong that they

are a threat to us. We must be prudent and
take steps against their increasing any further,
or if war should break out, they might add to
the number of our enemies. They might take
arms against us and so escape out of the country." Accordingly they put slave-drivers over the
Israelites to wear them down under heavy
loads. In this way they built the store-cities of
Pithom and Ramses for Pharaoh. But the more
they were crushed, the more they increased and
spread, and men came to dread the sons of
Israel. The Egyptians forced the sons of Israel
into slavery, and made their lives unbearable
with hard labor, work with clay and with brick,
all kinds of work in the fields; they forced on
them every kind of labor.[2]

This "king who knew nothing of Joseph" came from the ranks of
the native Egyptians who rebelled and finally threw off the foreign rulers,
beginning the period identified as the "New Kingdom" (1551-712 B.C.,
18th-24th Dynasties).

One of the kings of this period, Tuthmosis III, conquered Syria
and established Egyptian influence over what we now call the Bible lands;
his tomb is in the Valley of the Kings. Another strong character was
Ramesses II, the most celebrated of Egyptian kings. History shows that
along with defeating the Hittites, he was quite a builder, and his name is
found on almost every ancient Egyptian site. Despite this, in about 1285
B.C., he was beaten in a battle with the Hittites in northern Palestine,
and the boundaries of Egypt shrank considerably. Ramesses II is tradi-
tionally identified as the Pharaoh who oppressed the Israelites.

Perhaps it was the lost battle, the implied weakness, and the
internal dissension that signaled the time for the Israelites to rebel and
return to the land of Abraham and Sarah. Exodus identifies the leader

---

[2] *Exodus* 1:8-14.

of this movement as Moses, a man who not only had been adopted into the Egyptian court, but had significant relations with the Midianites of the Sinai desert.

The Midianites were descendants of Abraham's second wife, Keturah. This tribe also worshiped the same God as the Israelites, and Moses came back to Egypt convinced that this God had chosen him, in a dramatic way in the desert of the Sinai, to lead the Israelites to freedom. Note well that his time spent in the desert gave him both friends in that inhospitable land and a knowledge of the land and its features.

So, in about 1250 B.C. after a series of confrontations with the Pharaoh, Moses, Miriam and Aaron led their people out across the "Sea of Reeds," a marshy area near the Mediterranean coast. (The more dramatic notion that they crossed the Red Sea arose as a mistranslation of the text.) Exactly where they went as they wandered in the Sinai we do not know. They did, at some time, arrive at Mt. Sinai, some 7,500 feet high and part of a granite range at the southern end of the peninsula. There Moses received the vision of a covenant-making and covenant-keeping God, a vision that would control the destiny of his people ever after.

Sometime early in this period of wandering, they sent a spying party north into Canaan. The results were instructive; ten to two they decided that they were not up to fighting the natives for that land. It seems that these people, who had been so long oppressed by the Egyptians, had taken on an oppressed mentality. They had a poor self-image, we might say. The following years were a time when Moses and Joshua trained them to be guerilla fighters and to have a good self-image. We do not know exactly how much time is involved here, but scripture refers to it as forty years in the wilderness.

When they were ready, they moved north along the west side of the Dead Sea. Again this was not vacant territory. Moses first asked permission of the King of Edom to use the King's Highway, an ancient road still in existence. When he refused, Moses led them around the Edomites. Coming to the territory of the Amorites he again asked permission to cross, and again it was refused. This time the Amorite king sent an army to destroy the Israelites, and Moses and Joshua got to try out the new skills and identity they had learned in the wilderness. They defeated the Amorites and acquired the courage to go on to another successful engagement against another small kingdom.

Poised on the slopes of Mount Nebo, just 10 miles from where the Jordan River enters the Dead Sea, Moses called his people together for what would be his final message to them. Then Yahweh said to Moses:

> "This is the land I swore to give to Abraham, Isaac and Jacob, saying: I will give it to your descendants. I have let you see it with your own eyes, but you shall not cross into it." Thee in the land of Moab, Moses the servant of Yahweh died as Yahweh decreed. . . . Moses was a hundred and twenty years old when he died, his eye undimmed, his vigor unimpaired. The sons of Israel wept for Moses in the plains of Moab for thirty days. . . . Joshua, son of Nun was filled with the spirit of wisdom, for Moses had laid his hands on him. It was he that the sons of Israel obeyed, carrying out the order that Yahweh had given to Moses. [3]

So the mantle of leadership passed from Moses to Joshua, who undoubtedly was the person who had helped shape their new identity and given them such skills as they had to conquer the land before them. Joshua led them across the Jordan to Jericho and, after its fall, controlled the lower Jordan Valley. He then went up to the Judean hills, then on north. Finally the northern section of the land itself and Hazor, an ancient trading center, fell to his armies. Each of the twelve tribes were assigned a region and several chapters in the book of Joshua detail the boundaries.

But this should was not a conquest of the land in any complete sense. It neutralized the Canaanites by breaking up their coalitions. As

---

[3] *Deuteronomy* 34: 4-9.

a matter of fact the Israelites lived in a rather cozy relationship with the natives, borrowing their techniques of farming, their tools, and, too often, their gods.

Settling down in Canaan was a major move for these desert wanderers. From being nomads they suddenly had to become proficient at farming and flock keeping. Their political organization during this period was a confederacy of tribes. But, in addition to the heads of the tribes, there were individuals called "judges" who performed certain functions. This was a departure from the "head of the family/tribe/clan" pattern for these judges often were not such persons. The best description of the Judges is that they were local warlords, charismatic persons of unusual leadership ability. They could raise an army to put down rebellion on short notice or plan an expedition against some threatening nation.

The most pervasive threat came from the Philistines, a sea-people who had been repulsed from settling in the Delta section of Egypt and had landed on the coast further north. To this land they gave their name, translated later as Palestine. For centuries the Israelites would fight them whenever they moved inland from the coast toward the central highlands, the Negev, or the Valley of Jezreel.

There were other pressures as well, and these threats began to come so frequently that the people complained that they could not do their farming. They began to clamor for a more sophisticated political organization that would protect them. They observed that the Philistines, for instance, had kings and that these kings united the people in an effective way. So they began to push for a king as well. Samuel, the prophet, tried to tell them that they already had a king, Yahweh; but the people answered that was nice, but they wanted a king they could see.

The story of Samuel's attempt to dissuade them is told later in this book. He finally gave in and anointed Saul to be the first king of Israel. So the people made another major move in their growing identity. They were now a people with a monarchy, and they were united as never before, at least for a while.

Saul was not a very creative person. But he was followed by one of the most creative kings that Israel would ever know. David became king in about 1,000 B.C.. and in two astute political moves he united the nation. First he chose as his capital a town that was not special to any of the tribes and made it the center of government; that city is Jerusalem.

He then built a place for the Ark of the Covenant, the most visible part of the Israelite religion, and brought the Ark to Jerusalem. The people were required to worship there at least once each year and that, coupled with the usual need to come to the seat of government, quickly established Jerusalem as a very special place.

But it was David's son Solomon who gave Israel its largest borders and far flung trade routes, after he succeeded to the throne. Solomon inherited a united people and used them as a base to further the building of Jerusalem into a first-class city. He developed extensive trade connections both by land and sea and developed a copper industry from ore deposits in the Jordan Valley and in the area south of the Dead Sea. All this took money and labor, and Solomon got them by taxing the people.

Real tension arose within the Solomon's administration, and at least one officer, Rehoboam, had to flee to Egypt for his life. He came back when Solomon's son Jeroboam was about to be anointed king to replace his dead father. Rehoboam challenged Jeroboam and succeeded in getting the majority vote. Ten tribes supported him; only two went with Jeroboam. The result was that in 922 B.C., for the first time in their history, the Israelites were divided.

Once again Egypt played a role in this. A new pharaoh named Shishak seized the throne and began to dream of regaining possession of the Fertile Crescent. As we have said, he intervened in the politics of Solomon's court by giving refuge to Rehoboam and sending him back at the crucial moment. Solomon had been making preparations to defend his land against the Egyptians, and when Rehoboam took the throne he also had to do so. This gave Jeroboam time to consolidate his position in the north.

From this time onward, the ten tribes of the northern kingdom were known as *Israel*, while the two in the south were known as *Judah*. So the tribal people of Yahweh, oppressed in Egypt, molded into a fighting unit in the desert with a new identity, and victors over the Canaanites had become united. But the precarious unity that saw its greatest hope in David lasted only some seventy years and then broke apart, never to be healed again until the exile began about four centuries later.

The history of the people at this point is told in two ways: through the eyes of the prophets, and through the "official" documents in the books of Kings and Chronicles. The latter are largely a superficial listing of who was in power and tell us little of the actual lives of the people during this time. Kings came and went (sometimes in rapid succession), as did the kings of foreign nations. Egypt first reasserted control of Palestine, next Assyria under Ashurnasirpal, followed by Shalmaneser and Tiglath-pileser. The Assyrians were defeated by the Babylonians, and the Israelites had to deal with the mighty Nebuchadnezzar. Nebuchadnezzar invaded and destroyed Jerusalem in 586 B.C., sending into exile the remaining decision makers and important people. The northern kingdom had fallen earlier in about 722 B.C.

During all this, while the nation slid ever deeper into religious compromise and complacency, there was one bright moment; when Josiah became king, he valiantly attempted a rebellion and a return to a Mosaic understanding of the worship of the desert God, Yahweh. But in the end, it amounted to little, for the people were apathetic and the leaders downright corrupt.

Exile was a typical means of subjugation in those days. When one nation conquered another, the leaders, decision makers, image makers, artisans, and thinkers were usually taken back to the conquering country, where they could not foment rebellion and where they could enrich the conquering nation with their skills and talents. The peasants were left on the fields to provide income for the conquerors.

But a very important thing happened to our mothers and fathers in the faith as they sat "by the waters of Babylon" during the forty-eight years of exile. Led by the prophet Ezekiel and by the unnamed writer of II Isaiah (chapters 40-66), the people discovered that this God, Yahweh, who had led them out of bondage in Egypt, across the sea, and through the wilderness, and who gave them "the land of milk and honey," could be worshiped and understood anywhere, away from Jerusalem or any other center in Palestine. Further, they began to understand that this God Yahweh was a God of all nations, not just their own.

It was at this time that the priests took all the records of the people and put them together to form the Pentateuch as we know it today. They also wrote into the record certain blocks of material that justified their own existence as priests; in effect, they wrote their own job descriptions!

The time in Exile proved to be as much a watershed as did the Exodus. Both times were occasions for the people to examine and alter their identity, their self-image. During the Exodus they were transformed from a slave mentality to a fighting mentality; during the Exile they moved from thinking of themselves in a selfish way to a vision of themselves as a special people with a special task for the world of nations.

Once again, dramatic and far reaching movements of large masses of people had an effect on our mothers and fathers in the faith. The Fertile Crescent again erupted. Long dominated by one Semitic tribe of people after another, the region was suddenly invaded by Aryan-speaking people from the high plateau's of present day Iran; Cyrus the Persian conquered Babylon in about 539 B.C.

Cyrus had a different approach to conquered peoples. He released the Israelites and several other captured and exiled national groups to return to their homelands. These peoples were able to take back with them some of the treasures looted from them by the Babylonians, and they were given funds from the treasury to rebuild their cities and temples. Many Israelites returned in successive waves over several generations (the number given in the book of Ezra is 50,000). But a number decided to remain in Persia where they had done rather well economically, and some assumed places of power in Cyrus' administration.

Gradually, the walls and temple were rebuilt in Jerusalem, and a stable administration was put together with enough power to defend the city and the surrounding territory from various groups that had come into the land during the exile. The temple was completed and rededicated in 515 B.C.

Persia continued to prosper and to develop an impressive culture, but it would soon meet its match and more as the Greeks grew in strength.

The people of Israel (it is now possible to call them Jews, since essentially all that was left was the tribe of Judah) were not significant in world politics at this time. They fell silent, brooded, and filled the time by gathering and completing the written records of their pilgrimage from 1725 B.C. But swirling about them was the growing power of several potent nations. Greece fought Persia, and defeated it in several battles, most notably the Battle of Marathon in 490 B.C. Rome began to expand. In India, the Mauryan Empire began to expand, and in far away China, rebellions brought political chaos.

But it was the sudden appearance of a Greek named Alexander that stunned the world and our mothers and fathers in the faith. This twenty-year-old Macedonian seemed invincible; he stormed across the Hellespont into the Middle East and didn't stop until he controlled the land southward into Egypt and as far east as India.

The first book of the Maccabees in the *Apocrypha* sums up his career in vivid sentences:

> Alexander of Macedon, the son of Philip, marched from the land of Kittim, defeated Darius, king of Persia and Media, and seized his throne, being already king of Greece. In the course of many campaigns he captured fortified towns, slaughtered kings, traversed the earth to its remotest bounds, and plundered innumerable nations. when at last the world lay quiet under his rule, his pride knew no limits; he built up an extremely powerful army, and ruled over countries, nations and dominions; all paid him tribute.
>
> The time came when he fell ill, and, knowing that he was dying, he summoned his generals, nobles who had been brought up with him from childhood, and divided his empire among them while he was still alive. Alexander had reigned twelve years when he died. His general took over the government, each in his own province.

> On his death they were all crowned as kings,
> and their descendants succeeded them for many
> years. They brought untold miseries upon the
> world. [4]

In fact, when he died at thirty-three years of age, his generals divided up his empire and then fought among each other. In the process they destroyed the prosperity of the great trading ports of mainland Greece, and the center of wealth shifted to Alexandria, Egypt, where both Hellenistic and Jewish culture thrived. We should note at this point that the Jews were both numerous and prosperous in Alexandria. They were so influenced by the Greek culture there that they lost the use of the Hebrew language and the Old Testament had to be translated into Greek for their use.

Initially Palestine was assigned to the Ptolemies of Egypt and they were quite lenient in dealing with the Jews. But in 223 B.C. Antiochus III came to the Syrian throne in Antioch. He struck out at the Ptolemies and gained control of Palestine in 198 B.C. Unlike the Ptolemies, Antiochus III was a Hellenic ideologue. He aggressively promoted Hellenism and would accept no excuse for its not being the mode of the land.

His rise to power also disrupted a cozy relationship between the more wealthy Jews of the ruling class (basically in the cities) and the Egyptians. But in addition, Antiochus' promotion of Hellenism ran into strong resistance from a group of Jews known as the Hasidim. They were old-line, rigid conservatives, and when their devotion to Yahweh ran into the fanaticism of Antiochus' Hellenism, rebellion soon spread throughout the land of Palestine. The rebellion was not only against Hellenism, it was also a rebellion of conservative Jews against the liberals of the cities who had been living it up in collaboration with the Egyptians.

In the midst of the ensuing reign of terror, a rural man called Mattathias sparked the fight that would lead to Jewish independence. At his death in 166 B.C., his son Judas took over and was so successful

---

[4] *I Maccabees* 1:1-9.

against the Syrians that he came to be called "Maccabeus" which means "hammer." And hammer the Syrians he did. By this time, Rome was attacking the Greek Empire and was attempting to intervene in Middle Eastern affairs as well. This deflected attention to that greater problem and left the forces in Palestine much weaker than they would otherwise be. The rebellion succeeded and the Jews achieved a century of independence, but it was far from a peaceful time. Though the boarders of the land were extended back to what they had been in David's time, the land seethed with rivalries, and the factions fought bitterly for control.

Finally, exhausted by this civil war, the two major parties appealed for help to Rome, which by that time had taken over from the Greeks as "ruler of the world." Pompey was dispatched, entered Jerusalem in 63 B.C. and made Palestine part of the Roman province of Syria.

But peace was still not at hand. The Jews continued to fight among themselves. One of the faction leaders was Herod, son of Antipater, the procurator of the Jewish state. In another quarrel, Herod fled south for safety, then got himself to Rome and, with the help of other schemers, he got himself proclaimed King of Judaea by the Roman senate. With the help of Roman troops, he returned, captured Jerusalem after a siege of over two months, and was declared King in 37 B.C. His reign lasted until his death in 4 B.C.

During his reign, Herod did much building in Jerusalem. His finest achievement, which was also a great political accomplishment, was the rebuilding of the Great Temple on the very site where the old one had been destroyed. Not only did he build it, he built it according to all the various prescriptions of the Law. Nothing remains of this great temple except the vast terrace.

It was across this great terrace that Jesus of Nazareth first walked about ten years after the death of Herod. A few years later, Jesus would teach there, and it would be there that Jesus would eventually come to challenge the religious and political leaders of his day.

There was much unrest after the death of Herod. His successors simply were not skilled enough to govern such a cantankerous people. Of the seven people who held the chief administrative post, we know of only one, Pontius Pilate, who was procurator in the years 26-36 A.D.

Texts from that time show that thousands of Jews were crucified and over 30,000 were sold into slavery. Outbursts of demonstrations and outright rebellion were common. A group of Jews known to readers of the New Testament as Zealots (their name literally meant "stabbers") pledged to kill any disloyal Jew. They mingled in the streets, stabbed their victims, and disappeared in the resulting chaos. Rebellion continued all during the period and the 60,000 Roman troops under Vespasian found it difficult to deal with these fanatical rebels. The period is referred to in Roman history as the "Jewish War" (66-73 A.D.). When Vespasian was proclaimed emperor, he left his command to his son Titus. After five months of siege, Jerusalem fell and great atrocities committed by the Romans. The Jewish historian Josephus calculated that over a million Jews were killed during the siege and its aftermath. Some resistance continued until the fall of the desert fortress of Masada in 73 A.D.

Once more the temple was destroyed. The high priesthood and the Sanhedrin were abolished. The Sadducees who controlled the temple disappeared, and the Pharisees and the rabbis became the leaders of a worship which was then conducted exclusively in synagogues, a pattern that continues to our day.

There was one last rebellion in A.D. 132. Simeon Bar Cocheba, who claimed to be the Messiah, led a revolt and for three years fought off the Romans. He was finally defeated, and the record shows that 985 towns in Palestine were destroyed, some 580,000 men were killed, and nearly all of Judea was laid waste.

The Jewish state would not be independent again until 1948.

Chapter Two

EAST OF EDEN

The educational techniques used by our mothers and fathers in the faith over 4,000 years ago were absolutely phenomenal. They knew then what many of us have only recently discovered, that the great and deep issues of life, the value scales we care about most, can be taught best by way of a story.

Those were great and grand and glorious days for storytelling, 4,000 years ago, for there were no printing presses; people relied upon their memories and their storytelling abilities to pass their tradition from one generation to another. It was done with the vibrancy of creative language around the campfire as they traveled, not with dry words on a written page.

The ancient bards wandered the land telling their stories, teaching the issues of life. They would gather the people about them, have them sit down to listen, and say: "Once upon a time. . ."

Today we have a story of two brothers, Cain and Abel, but this is only the first of several stories that tell of two brothers; later on we shall hear of Jacob and Esau and of the two lost sons.

The story in the Bible just before the one of Cain and Abel is that of Adam and Eve. The story of Adam and Eve deals with the vertical crisis of alienation between humans and God, while the story of Cain and Abel and the other "brother" stories deal with horizontal crises of alienation between humans. They raise the question of how we get along with one another.

Listen now to this story of two brothers, Cain and Abel. They grew to manhood and earned their living by different means. Cain by farming, Able by tending flocks. Nothing novel here, but the plot begins to thicken when they bring their offerings to the altar of God.

Cain brought the first fruits of the soil; what else could he bring? Abel brought the first fruits of the flock; what else could he bring? But scripture says that Yahweh looked with favor on Able and his offering;

but he did not look with favor on Cain and his offering. The result was that Cain was led to resentment, envy, and (eventually) to murderous rage. Exactly why one offering was acceptable to Yahweh and the other was not is never explained, but to get tied up in a discussion of this is to miss the point of the story.

There is a famous painting of Cain and Abel in Florence, Italy. It is done in vivid colors, and I can still see the dark frown on Cain's face as he watches the smoke from Abel's offering go straight up to heaven, while that from Cain's flattens out over the ground.

Not only was Cain angry, he stayed angry, and nothing God could do made him feel any better about it. God made very clear his concern over Cain's anger and his continuing concern for Cain. "Why are you angry," said Yahweh,[1] "why has your countenance fallen? You're OK Cain. I love you."

But Cain could not accept that love. Cain wanted to have happen to him exactly what happened to his brother. He wanted to be accepted exactly as his brother had been accepted. He wanted to jump through the same hoops; he wanted the same dividends. Yahweh warned him about his attitude, warned him that his resentment would eat his insides out. Yahweh used a graphic illustration to make the point.

> Cain, be careful, your resentment is lying around waiting to eat you out inside like a crouching beast that lies outside your door ready to rush in, grab you and eat you. You either rule that beast or it will rule you. Get your anger under control, Cain.

Note that sin is here portrayed as an aggressive force ready to ambush Cain. Sin is larger than Cain; it takes on a life of its own; it is lethal. The teaching here is that we must be on guard; sin is in our

---

[1] I usually use the term "Yahweh" when referring to the specific Judaic/Christian God of our tradition. This is the best translation of the Hebrew word in the Old Testament and was the word used to describe this particular God as contrasted with a generic reference to god.

hands, not some blind destiny; sin can be ruled. Remember John Steinbeck's nobel prize winning novel *East of Eden*? The major theme of the novel revolved around this verse in Genesis, and Steinbeck interprets it in the book. Listen as the character Adam Trask speaks:

> There was only one place that bothered me. The King James Version says this; it is when Jehovah has asked Cain why he is angry. Jehovah says, "If thou doest well, shalt thou not be accepted? And if thou doest not well, sin lieth at the door. And unto thee shall be his desire, and *thou shalt* rule over him." It was the "thou shalt" that struck me, because it was a promise that Cain would conquer sin. . . . Then I got a copy of the American Standard Bible. It was very new then. And it was different in this passage. It says . . . "do thou rule over him." Now this is very different. This is not a promise, it is an order. And I began to stew about it. I wondered what the original word of the original writer had been. . . .
>
> It is easy out of laziness, out of weakness, to throw oneself onto the lap of the deity, saying, "I couldn't help it; the way was set." But think of the glory of the choice! That makes a man a man. A cat has no choice, a bee must make honey. There's no godliness there. . . .
>
> This is a ladder to climb to the stars. . . . You can never lose that. It cuts the feet from under weakness and cowardliness and laziness . . . I feel that I am a man. And I feel that a man is a very important thing; maybe more important than a star. This is not theology. I have no bent towards gods. But I have a new love for that glittering instrument, the human soul. It is a lovely and unique thing in the uni-

verse. It is always attacked and never destroyed; because, "thou mayest."[2]

Steinbeck correctly perceives that the key is the phrase "thou
mayest." To Steinbeck's hero, and to us, it is an invitation, a challenge,
and a promise. Sin can be ruled; anger can be ruled.

But Cain was angry and hurt, and he refused to be either
placated or warned. He nursed his hurt pride until it poisoned the
deepest wells of his being and darkened every horizon of his life. Hurt
became anger, anger became suspicion, suspicion became malice, and
malice laid the blame on innocent Able and led to a plan to destroy him.

We're all familiar with how much we may dislike persons who
seem to walk serenely among us, having it altogether; how much we
sometimes want to rattle their cages or topple them down; how much it
may torment us, like a wild beast gnawing at the vitals of a living animal.

Cain goes into the field and quarrels with Abel and kills him.
Upon returning home, Cain pretends he does not know where Abel is.

"Am I my brothers keeper?" he demanded to know. He got his
answer fast enough. It was the same answer we have been getting to that
question from that day to this: "You bet your life you are."

Cain may have denied that he was his brother's keeper but he
could not deny that he was his brother's slayer. He could not keep the
blood of his slain brother from crying out to Yahweh against him; he
couldn't dodge responsibility for it and couldn't avoid punishment for it.
Cain was a marked person from that day on. Is it a mark we all bear?

Back to John Steinbeck's novel, *East of Eden*. In it, Steinbeck
portrays a drama of good and evil in the souls of all persons, a modern
interpretation of the eternal story of Cain and Abel. It is fundamentally
a search into the cost and the causes of conflict between persons who are
or ought to be close to each other. But they wander estranged, East of
Eden. Steinbeck took a whole novel to say it. Genesis compresses it into
two dozen verses.

It begins with the fact that occasions for hurt pride and anger lie
about each one of us each day. Inevitably they involve friends, col-

---

[2] John Steinbeck, *East of Eden*, Viking Press, 1952, NY, pp. 301-304.

leagues, and loved ones. They involve members of our families. They involve people we scarcely know. How to react to them wisely is one of the permanent problems of life. There is surely a right and a wrong way to do it, and Cain choose the wrong one. Instead of keeping in mind the blamelessness of Abel and the reassurance of God that he, Cain, was dear to him, Cain was blinded by his hurt pride and his anger. He was blinded to his lifelong ties to Abel, blinded to God's promise and warning.

So self-pity became self-righteousness. His suspicions found malicious plots in every action and every word of Abel. He became paranoid, and he poisoned himself mentally, emotionally, and spiritually. He found malice and slights where there were none. On edge with expectation of trouble, he found trouble everywhere because he brought trouble with him wherever he went. It may come down to a fact as simple as this: Cain could not stand to see anyone get ahead of him, not even his own brother, in whose welfare he should have rejoiced.

It was not enough that God told Cain again and again of his care for him in many concrete ways. No, Cain had to have it in every way that Able had it or he couldn't live with Abel. So the second movement in this very old and ever new story finds Cain sealing his own fate, as well as Abel's, by his refusal to heed either the promise or the warning of God.

And so the deed was done. Cain killed Abel. By doing so, he set in motion a train of forces over which he no longer had control. Right at the point where Cain planned to get complete control of the situation, to right his wrongs, to set things right, he lost control completely and finally.

Cain tried to play innocent, but soon found out the futility of that. He was hauled to his feet, stood against the wall of hard fact, and made to accept full moral responsibility for what he had done.

God's judgment fell like a trip-hammer, destroying the form and pattern of Cain's life. To Cain the farmer, he said: "The very earth curses you, it will no longer yield to your efforts to farm it." To Cain the man with parents and home, he said: "Hence forth you are to be a fugitive, a vagabond on the earth."

Thus Cain had his moment of truth, too late to avert tragedy, but not too late to know it when it came for what it was. There are few

sadder words in the Old Testament than these: "My punishment is
greater than I can bear."

Hurt pride and anger that were permitted to become so strong that
they took control of Cain's feelings, judgments, and actions led to murder. They cost Cain and Abel their love for each other; they cost Abel
his life; they cost Cain his home.

Brooding over this narrative, we become aware of the tragedy
of loss, separation, and estrangement of each of us from one another and
from our creator. As we face ourselves today in the light of this story,
who can help but confess that we, like Cain, are caught up in the causes
and cost of this kind of conflict in many desperate and unsolved ways.
Honesty should keep us from leveling a finger of blame at Cain, for each
of us can supply evidence of our own guilt. Even if we have not actually
killed someone as Cain killed Abel, have we not permitted slights and
indignities, intentional or not, to poison our lives, distort our relationships, and darken the horizons of our lives. With the cost of conflict
higher than ever, we may well wonder about the cost of a cure, if cure
there be.

Both Genesis and the New Testament agree there is a cure!
Listen to Yahweh. "Learn my way and keep it." It's the New Testament
that spells out the way to keep the way of God. We don't like to hear
it, for it runs against our present propaganda. Jesus said we must love
our enemies, pray for them, and seek to help them in such a fashion as
to emphasize our unity and our affection for them.

The writer of I John explicitly uses the brother theme when he
writes that "he who says he loves God but hates his brother is a liar."
Augustine said that love of enemy is the summit of Christian virtue, and
it is. It alone will keep us from being blinded by hatred, self-pity, and
self-righteousness. It alone will keep us humble enough to hear and heed
the voice of God. There is no other way. Whether we take it and travel
toward life, or reject it and travel toward death is the choice we must
make.

It is a great cost laid upon us for we are called to exhibit *agape*
love. *Agape* is not a cheap, selfish, or judgmental love. It is a radical
love because it is non-reciprocal in its outreach. It gives and expects
nothing in return. It is a love that is goes out to all, even the not friend-

ly, the unlovable. It begins right at home when members of our own families are most unlovable, because that is when they need us to love them most. In the midst of my Cainness is when I most need someone to surround me with *agape* love, and when I most need to remind myself of the *agape* love that does surround me from a God who is that *agape* love always.

So the ancient story tells of the causes and cost of conflict and points to Jesus who, caught in conflict, demonstrates the cure of conflict: "Love one another as I have loved you!"

*   *   *   *   *

The story of Cain and Able is found in *Genesis*, chapter 4.

Chapter Three

RAM IN THE THICKET,
LAMB ON THE THRONE

The first eleven chapters of the Bible cover more than eleven million years of history; now that's tight writing. The theme of these chapters is Yahweh's relationship not just to Adam and Eve, or Cain and Able, but to all persons. There is only brief reference to art, industry, and science in these writings and they say nothing at all of the great civilizations that developed in the Nile and Euphrates valleys. The one real concern is with the spiritual development of human beings.

We first read how Yahweh made all things good, creating humans to "image" or to make concrete in our relations the love which is the essence of God. We are told how humans fell out of that relationship and became alienated from each other and from Yahweh.

In the story of Cain and Able we find evidence that the alienation of Adam and Eve from each other and from Yahweh goes even further, "Am I my brother's keeper?" asks Cain. Created for fellowship, he falls further into alienation. In the very asking of the question is a denial of responsibility.

Then comes the story of the flood, Yahweh's attempt to begin all over again. But, after the flood, nothing has changed. Alienation reappears in the family of Noah and once more spreads throughout the earth. There follows the story of the Tower of Babel which pictures the revolt of civilized people against Yahweh. The story of the confusion of tongues is not a scientific account of the beginning of various languages, but a dramatic pictorial presentation of the truth that growing human impiety toward Yahweh had brought confusion and discord into all relationships. Thus, the last thread binding humans together is destroyed and chaos is back again; humans are estranged from each other and from the Creator God.

But now comes a radical change in the writing of the Old Testament. Chapter 12 is yet another new beginning and provides a new focus in which we move from human beings in general to two human beings in particular, from all humankind to the story of Abraham and Sarah.

This is the great dividing place in the Bible. The majority of the human race, alienated from Yahweh, continue building towers, speaking against heaven, and building cities with the thought that they will last forever; but the Bible tells us Yahweh now began to gather a special people, a people of faith. The one who called the world into being now makes a second call.

This second call is specific, and it's object is identifiable in history. It is the first truly historical statement in the Bible and is addressed to a man named Abraham and a woman named Sarah; the purpose of the call is to fashion an alternative community in a creation gone awry.

Chapter eleven of Genesis is a table of the descendants of the family after the flood and is as dull as the phone book. It lists the genealogy of several dozen families and comes down to Sarah and Abraham; there it cryptically states that "Sarah was barren, having no child." Period.

This statement is both cryptic and descriptive. To begin a new history of humankind, I would have done it in a more hopeful context. But not Yahweh. Yahweh inexplicably speaks his powerful word into the midst of barrenness. That is the good news! That is the ground of hope! Yahweh calls the hopeless ones into a community. Yahweh calls the fixed ones into a pilgrimage. The command to Abraham and Sarah is terse; John Calvin translated it as "Go, with eyes closed, having renounced thy country. Thou shalt have given thyself wholly to me."

Ah ha! Departure from security is the only way out of barrenness. To stay in safety is to remain barren; to leave and to risk is to have hope. And suddenly there comes to mind the statement of Jesus that "whoever would save his life must loose it, and who looses it for my sake and the gospel's will save it." Do we genuinely want to be out of our barrenness? Perhaps renunciation is too great a cost?

There is one last point before we go into the story itself; in this story we find that faith is described, not defined. Faith is like a man called Abraham. Here are the opening verses:

> Yahweh said to Abraham, "Leave your country, your family and your father's house for the land I will show you. I will make you a great nation. I will bless you and make your name so famous that it will be used as a blessing. I will bless those who bless you. I will curse those who slight you. All the tribes of the earth shall bless themselves by you. . . . So Abraham went as Yahweh told him, and Lot went with him. Abraham was seventy-five years old when he left Haran. Abraham took with him his wife Sarah, his nephew Lot, and all the possessions they had amassed and the people they had acquired in Haran. They set off for the land of Canaan and arrived there." [1]

Note that the metaphor is of a journey. The life of faith is characterized as a journey. It is a challenge to the dominant ideologies of our time (and of Abraham's) which yearn for settlement, security, and placement.

Now walk with the man and woman in the story. They went out from their homeland not knowing exactly where they were going. They left the familiar and took the risk of going into the unknown. They walked about 1,000 miles. It was slow going, and it must have been a mob scene to rival a Barnum and Bailey Circus parade. There would have been family, relatives, servants, cattle, sheep, goats, and chickens (you had to take along the groceries for the trip), and you had to go

---

[1] *Genesis* 12:1-5.

where the animals could be grazed and watered. There was also the baggage.

Finally they arrived in the land promised to them, but it was not vacant land, and the residents took a dim view of these intruders. Furthermore, it was not a well-watered land but a fragile land where famine was common.

Then the writer shows us by several illustrations that Abraham was not a perfect person. After they arrive in Canaan there is famine and Abraham's faith grows weak. They leave and go to Egypt for food, where they find a civilization as old and wicked as the one they left. Fearful for his own life, Abraham lies about Sarah being his wife and lets Pharaoh take her from him for his own. Here is the text:

> On the threshold of Egypt, Abraham said to his wife Sarah, "Listen, I know you are a beautiful woman. When the Egyptians see you they will say, 'That is his wife,' and they will kill me but spare you. Tell them you are my sister, so that they may treat me will because of you and spare my life out of regard for you.
>
> When Abraham arrived in Egypt the Egyptians did indeed see that thee woman was very beautiful. When Pharaoh's officials saw her they sang her praises to Pharaoh and the woman was taken into Pharaoh's palace. He treated Abraham well because of her, and he received flocks, oxen, donkeys, men and women slaves, she-donkeys and camels. But yahweh inflicted severe plagues on Pharaoh and his household because of Abraham's wife Sarah. So Pharaoh summoned Abraham and said, "What is this you have done to me? Why did you not tell me she was your wife? Now, here is your wife. Take her and go!" Pharaoh committed him to men

who escorted him back to the frontier with his
wife and all he possessed.[2]

A sad story of the lack of faith, and this is followed by another illustration.

Strife arose between the herdsmen of Abraham and those of Lot over possession and use of fertile fields and easy water. Abraham resolves the issue by offering his nephew Lot first choice of the land. It does not take Lot long to decide; he takes a look at the Jordan River valley, irrigated everywhere like the garden of Eden and chooses all the Jordan for himself. He leaves the barren hills to his uncle. But Yahweh again comes into the picture. Yahweh is now pleased with Abraham's style, an honest, faithful style, and he blesses Abraham.

In these two illustrations we see the humanness of Abraham. In Egypt his faith is weak, he doubts the promise, and gets into trouble; in the second scene his faith is strong, he believes the promise, and he is blessed and prospers.

But the greatest test of Abraham's faith comes in chapter 22, one of the most poignantly touching scenes in all of literature as far as I am concerned. Yahweh promises again and again to make of them a great nation, but Abraham responds in frustration, "Yahweh you keep saying that, but as yet, not even one child!" And the years passed. Then, when Sarah was ninety [imagine, ninety years of age!] visitors came to their tent and promised that she would bear a child. How she laughed at the thought. But she bore a son, and they named him Isaac, which means, literally, "he laughs." So Yahweh had the last laugh, when Mr. Laughter himself was born nine months later.

We come at last to the magnificent chapter 22. Yahweh says,

Take your son, your only child Isaac, whom you
love, and go offer him as a burnt offering on a
mountain I will point out to you.

---

2 *Genesis* 12:10-20.

Can you imagine the anguish, even though child sacrifice was actually a common thing in those days and in those lands? (They saw a parallel between offering to the gods the first fruit of the land and the first fruit of a woman; through this they expected to find protection and blessing.) But, to sacrifice this child! The one for whom they had waited so long! The one promised! Kill Isaac? No descendants? No future? Back to barrenness? The entire pilgrimage for naught? Abraham has trusted the promise fully. Now the promise is to be abrogated.

But the story goes on without interruption:

> Rising early next morning, Abraham saddled his
> ass and took with him two of his servants and
> his son Isaac.

The intended sacrifice rides, the father walks leading the animal. Does that remind you of Jesus riding on the ass into Jerusalem centuries later, the intended sacrifice for the sin of the world? The whole story reeks of the attitude of a loving father. They arrive, and Abraham loads the wood for the sacrifice fire onto Isaac to carry up the mountain, while he takes the dangerous material, the knife and the fire. Again my mind races ahead centuries, Jesus carries the wooden cross upon which he will be killed.

Off they go up the mountain. The language is "hand in hand as one person." The ascent is a torturous one. Then comes the long overdue question. "Father," said Isaac. "Yes, my son," Abraham repled. "Look here are the fire and the wood, but where is the lamb for the burnt offering?" And Abraham replies, "My son, God himself will provide the lamb for the burnt offering." And then the phrase again, they go off hand in hand as one person. They reach the top and a rude altar is constructed. The hands of Abraham must have shaken as he rolls together the stones and piles on the wood. Then he places his child, his only child, on the wood and raises his hand which clutches the knife.

Then the voice of Yahweh. "Abraham, Abraham." "Yes, I am here." "Do not raise your hand against the boy!" And Abraham looks up through tear stained eyes and there, caught in the thicket is a ram. He seizes it and sacrifices it in place of his son.

The lesson here, which is never forgotten by Israel, is that human sacrifice is not acceptable to Yahweh. Our God of love is revolted by it. But, the almost sacrifice of Isaac, halted at the last moment, was the beginning of a slow ascent toward another sacrifice. That sacrifice would go on to the end, for there would be no ram in the thicket to take the place of the victim; that sacrifice would take place centuries later in the same general piece of geography; in place of the ram, it would be the lamb, the Lamb of God, who takes away the sin of the world.

Despite his age, Abraham was a novice in faith, not perfect, not a possessor of a full grown faith at all. Many, many times during his life he must have wanted to quit. But, like a child, he had the openness and the wonder to take a risk. That openness, that willingness to keep on trying to understand, permitted Yahweh to surround him with his care and concern and give him a glimpse of the very nature of God as love. So Abraham comes down to us through the centuries as a beautiful person who illustrated faith.

The extensive folklore developed around Ignace Paderewski, the famous Polish concert pianist and prime minister, includes the following story. A mother who wished to encourage her young son's study of the piano, bought tickets for a performance by Paderewski. When the great night arrived, they found their seats near the front of the concert hall and eyed the majestic piano waiting on stage. Soon the mother found a friend to talk to, and the boy slipped away. When the time of the performance arrived, the houselights dimmed, the audience quieted, the spotlights came on, and only then did they notice the boy up on the bench innocently picking out, "Twinkle, twinkle, little star." His mother gasped, but before she could retrieve her son, the master appeared on the stage and quickly moved to the keyboard. "Don't quit, keep playing," he whispered to the boy. Leaning over, Paderewski reached down with his left hand and began filling in a bass part. Soon his right arm reached around the other side, encircling the child, to add a running obligato. Together, the old master and the young novice held the crowd mesmerized.

In our lives, unpolished though we may be, it is our loving Yahweh who surrounds us and whispers in our ear time and again,

"Don't quit, keep playing." And as we do, God augments and supple-
ments until a work of amazing beauty is created, and we too, like Abraham are judged as persons of faith.

*   *   *   *   *

The story of Abraham is found in *Genesis*: 12-24.

Chapter Four

YOU CAN'T SLEEP ON
ROCKS FOREVER

Some of you may have enjoyed, as I did, the marvelous English stage production "Beyond the Fringe". There's one scene in the play in which Alan Bennet gives a mock sermon that is absolutely hilarious (at least I thought so), but which a lot of people thought was serious. Unfortunately, I've heard many preachers give sermons just like it.

Alan Bennet comes onto the stage alone, a tight little man dressed as an English cleric, and says:

> The eleventh verse of the twenty-seventh chapter of the Book of Genesis: "My brother Esau is an hairy man, but I am a smooth man." Now there come times in the lives of each and every one of us when we turn aside from our fellows and seek the solitude and tranquility of our own firesides. When we put up our feet and put on our slippers and sit and stare into the fire. I wonder, at such times, whether your thoughts turn, as mine do, to those words I've just read for you now: "My brother Esau is an hairy man, but I am a smooth man."
>
> As I was on my way here to speak I arrived at the station and by an oversight I happened to come out by the way one is supposed to go in. And as I was coming out, causing a great disruption in the flow of people, an employee of the railway company hailed me: "Hey, mate,"

he shouted, "where do you think you are going?" That at any rate was the gist of what he
said.

You know, I was grateful to him, because, you
see, he put me in mind of the kind of question
I felt I ought to be asking you here this day.
Where do you think you're going?[1]

Alan Bennet goes on with this inept sermon (probably modeled on one
he had heard) and concludes with:

So now I draw to a close. I want you to go
out into the world, in times of trouble and
sorrow and helplessness and despair amid the
hurly-burly of modern life. And if ever you are
tempted to say: "Oh, shove this!" I want you to
remember for comfort the words of my text to
you, "My brother Esau is an hairy man but I am
a smooth man."

I am not going to do exactly that, but I do want to deal with
Jacob and Esau and with the question, "Hey, mate, just where do you
think you are going?"

Isaac and Rebekah had twin sons who were rivals from birth.
The first born was named Esau, which means red, because his body was
crimson under a growth of thick dark hair. His brother's skin was a
gentler pink and as hairless as the palm of his hand. Because he had
seized his brothers heel, trying to come out first, he was named Jacob,
which means "a wrestler" or "one who supplants."

Esau, the rugged firstborn, grew up to be his fathers' favorite,
though in his love for hunting and vigorous activity, his careless, happy
ways, and his independent but generous ideas, Esau was really quite
unlike his father Isaac. Isaac was a kindly, quiet, and meditative person.
Theirs was an attraction of opposites. Esau would come back from the

---

[1]   Alan Bennett, *Beyond the Fringe; A Review*, S. French, London, 1963, p.43.

chase and regale his doting father with tales of adventure and bold exploits, and he always brought home meat for his father.

Jacob was quite otherwise. He seemingly had no adventure in him, but was content to be a shepherd and a farmer with time to think. From earliest childhood, Jacob was adored by Rebekah, his mother, and she dominated him while watching Esau with a critical eye. Because Esau was the first born, by law and custom he had the birthright, the most important thing a man could inherit. But the birthright was also a great moral responsibility, a sacred obligation imposed on every firstborn son. It carried priestly privileges and responsibilities in the family, including the necessity to decide all disputes wisely and with prayer and the leading of the family in serving God.

But Esau was obviously not the priestly type. All he wanted was to chase wild beasts and tell wild stories. Only by accident had Esau been born first; by natural ability and the knack of real leadership, Jacob felt he should have had the birthright. If by some decree he had been able to get it, everybody would have been better off, including Esau, who had no desire to be bothered with responsibility.

It would be easy for us to fall into the usual routine at this point in the story, condemning Jacob for his craftiness, and loveing Esau because he was the underdog. But look for a minute at this twin Esau. What was the matter with him? Why didn't he play a great role in Israel's spiritual history? His difficulty was that he lived only in the immediate moment and by the light of what was obvious. When Esau was hungry he wanted to eat, right then. When he was sleepy he wanted to sleep, right then. When he wanted adventure, he hunted, right then. Never any thought about tomorrow, next week, next year. But not so Jacob. He thought about the future, tomorrow, next week, next year.

Esau was heir to the birthright, and it meant a great deal if you looked far enough ahead. But to Esau it meant nothing. Its benefits were intangible and seemed a long way off; they did not fill the stomach when it was empty.

And so one day it happened. Jacob was cooking a pot of lentil stew over a fire in the field when a shadow suddenly covered his hands. It was bother Esau, exhausted after a long, unlucky hunt. The red-haired brother threw his enormous body down on the ground; his good-natured eyes looked hungrily at the food, his nostrils sniffed its delicate fragrance. "I'm starved," he said in mock despair, "how about some stew brother dear?" Jacob shook his head, "There is just enough for one and I am famished too after having worked the field all day." Esau would have had to walk several more miles to home, where dinner would be waiting. "But brother, I'm hungry now. I'd give all I own for that dish of stew." And that was it. Jacob's fingers interlaced, "Well, how about selling the birthright?" Esau laughed when he heard the proposition. Why not? Who wanted to be the family leader in prayer anyway? And the transaction was made. Jacob was happy with the birthright, and Esau was happy with his stew.

Esau showed that he did not care enough for life's great possibilities to pay the price of present discipline. He must have what he wanted, when he wanted it, and consequences could go hang. That was the critical weakness of Esau, and that was his condemnation. He lost tomorrow because he snatched so greedily at today.

But there is a second instance in the life of these two brothers where Jacob's culinary art comes to the fore. Day by day Rebekah and Jacob watched the old man Isaac grow weaker and more helpless. Then toward the end, Isaac called Esau to his side and said:

> See, I am old, and I do not know when I may
> die. Now take your weapons, your quiver and
> bow, and go out to the field, and hunt game for
> me, and prepare for me some savory food, that
> I may eat and bless you before I die. [2]

Rebekah overheard that conversation with Esau, and, while Jacob had managed to cook Esau out of his birthright alone, his mother Rebekah is the moving spirit in the theft of the blessing. She told Jacob what she had heard and then ordered: "Now my son, obey my voice and do what I command you."

The authority of a mother's affection many turn a child to goodness; misused it may involve him in evil for which he will pay a

---

[2] *Genesis* 27: 1-4.

heavy price. Rebekah could make a decision for Jacob but she could not take upon herself the debt of retribution that would be involved.

The story is vividly told. It's pitiful that the blurred eyes, dimmed ears, and even the once-sensitive fingers of the old man Isaac could no longer distinguish the favorite son from the scheming brother. Jacob rushed out and killed a young goat from the nearby flock, and, with his mother's help, he spices it in the pot so that it tastes like game. He then puts on Esau's smelly clothes and wraps his arms in goatskins to counterfeit the hairiness of Esau. And it works! Jacob gets the blessing.

The discovery of Jacob's trickery is one of the most pathetic scenes in the Bible. Isaac is dismayed but resigned, the blessing has been spoken and there is no bringing it back. Esau is shocked and unable to believe that the blessing, once within his grasp, has now slipped away. Rebekah would soon be dead and gone. But Jacob will have to live for years in the same world with the brother he has defrauded. And he will have to live with himself.

But he was in serious danger of not living very much longer at all, for Esau's hatred became so intense that he vowed that when his father Isaac died he would murder his tricky brother. That was when Jacob left home. Again it was Rebekah who thought up the plan and it was a plausible and valid one. She proposed that, like his father, Jacob should have a wife from among their own people in northwest Mesopotamia. So Jacob set off to obtain a wife. He starts out as a lonely traveler on a mission of uncertain outcome. The young man who had depended so much on his mother goes forth from beneath her protecting care. Although she tells him that it will be but a few days and that when his brother's wrath subsides she will send for him to come back, he knows that it will be a long time. In fact, the time was twenty years, and his mother was evidently dead and buried before he came back.

So Jacob, the civilized man, who liked the comfort of a tent, must now seek rest where he can find it, laying down at night in the rocky fields. Jacob, the domestic man who cooked the savory stew, must now depend on what he can obtain en route. Jacob, the quiet man, must now go out into the rough world.

The way was long. On a map the distance is about 400 miles of rugged terrain and severe climate. Several nights from home, out in a field, the lone wanderer made his camp. He took a stone, put it under his head, and lay down to sleep. Such a barren spot was an unlikely place for anything special to happen, and Jacob was an unlikely enough person to whom anything special might happen. After all, he had deceived his father, defrauded his brother, and by his own words he was not expecting anything special to happen.

But something did happen. Something unexpected and wonderful. Jacob dreamed and in his dream he saw a ladder set up on earth and the top reached to heaven. The angels of God were ascending and descending it and Yahweh stood above it and said, "I am the God of Abraham and Isaac. . . ." And Yahweh renewed the covenant promise to Jacob that the land would belong to him and to his descendants for he was the one who received the birthright and the blessing.

And Jacob woke up and said: "Surely the Lord was in this place and I did not know it." And the place was suddenly awesome. He set up the stone he had been sleeping on as a memorial and consecrated it by pouring oil on it. And he called the place, Beth el, which means "House of God."

But like so many of us, even this dream, this consciousness of God's presence, did not effect Jacob's life very long. He still reserved part of his old nature, he was not totally committed. He went on from Bethel to labor with his uncle Laban, and so crafty and shrewd was he that he came off with two wives, a money inheritance, men servants, maid servants, and a great herd of cattle! Not bad for a refugee. He hadn't lost his touch. He feathered his own nest well, taking advantage of all the law allowed and perhaps some in addition, if he could get away with it.   But Jacob longed for home, so one day he started the journey back. But the closer he got, the more he thought of Esau. And the more he thought of Esau, the more afraid he became.

Then came the word that Esau was coming to meet him! It's interesting to note the extravagant preparations Jacob made to appease his brothers wrath. Scripture says:

> From what he had with him he chose a gift for
> his brother Esau: two hundred she-goats and
> twenty he-goats, two hundred ewes and twenty

rams, thirty camels in milk with their calves, forty cows and ten bulls, twenty she-asses and ten donkeys.[3]

He was willing to divest himself of all his gains just to be at peace with his brother again. After all these years he still had a felling of guilt about his brother, and about his God, Yahweh!

Ah, that was it! He had offended Yahweh also! So on his way to appease his brother, Jacob must also deal with his God. It must have been this realization that prompted him, on the last night, to send everyone else ahead while he remained behind to think things out for himself. Maybe his mind went back to the night at Beth el when he was alone before and felt in touch with God. So Jacob laid down that night on the rocks by the brook Jabbok. And once again something happened. It is described as Jacob wrestling with an angel. A very different experience than the one at Beth el. There the vision of God had come to Jacob as a benediction, now the reality of God had to be encountered in another and more awful way.

Jacob had to wrestle with the dreadful mystery of existence, and it was a costly encounter with God, a deep searching of the heart, a longing for a new way of life, for a conversion of the old into the new. And it proved very painful. He limped forever afterward, says the Bible. The experience had left him a marked man. Such a real encounter is always difficult for the prodigal, and something really happened to Jacob this time. It is signified by his new name. No longer is he called Jacob, but Israel.

Jacob would never walk again in lofty arrogance, never again be the cheat, the deceiver, the crafty one. For now he had a destiny. Out of that strange wrestling Jacob became a new man, a different person. One immediate proof of the change was the absence of all fear of Esau's vengeance. Calmly he waits the meeting and its consequence.

He watched a cloud of dust approach far down the road. He soon saw Esau riding at the head of a galloping column of 400 men! Brother Esau rode on a swift camel, red hair flying in the wild wind, one

---

[3] *Genesis* 32:15-17.

arm out high and eager. But it was empty; there was no sword in that hand. Instead it was a palm exposed in friendship.

The twins met and embraced! Esau received Jacob as the father did the prodigal son in Jesus' story. And the emptiness in the pit of Jacob's stomach was no more. Jacob was reconciled not only to his bother but to God as well.

That is what I like about the Old Testament, it is full of hope for us all! Just look at Jacob. Haven't you had the experience of selling your future for a mess of stew? Haven't you had the experience of cheating someone out of something that is theirs by right? Haven't you had a Beth el experience when you flee from another's wrath and feel good that God still cares about you? Haven't you had the experience of going right back to the same old way of life, even taking pride in the shrewd deals you cook up? Haven't you really cried out for a change in character, for a new opportunity, for a new life? Well you too can have a Jabbok experience. You too can come to grips with yourself and Yahweh.

Open yourself to the wrestling with your soul that has been so long awaiting. Wrestle as Jacob did and you too may well find it painful enough to make you limp the rest of your life. But you can't sleep on rocks forever. Wrestle, but then get up and once more engage life and discover a new perspective.

*   *   *   *   *

The story of Jacob and Esau is told in *Genesis*, chapter 25:19 through chapter 33:17.

Chapter Five

MOSES: THE FIRST HUMAN RIGHTS ACTIVIST

Perhaps I've bit off more than I can chew to try to tell the story of Moses in one sermon! It is an epic story about an heroic person set against a vast canvas. The time was about 1250 B.C.

At that time, people were spreading by the millions all over the face of the earth. In the Far East, the Hsia dynasty had come to power and was laying the foundation of a Chinese empire, and the Aryan invasion was sweeping down the snowy mountains passes of Northern India. On green islands in the Aegean Sea, Greek culture was beginning. The pyramids in Egypt were already 1,300 years old when Yahweh said, "I send you, Moses, to Pharaoh to being the sons and daughters of Israel, my people, out of Egypt."

Slow of speech, this lonely shepherd drew back in anguish at the command of God. He was uncertain if the people would support him if he challenged the mightiest monarch on earth. Small wonder that he hesitated, but he had the might of Yahweh behind him, and, before the sands ran out for him at the age of one hundred and twenty, he had tumbled Pharaoh, led the Israelites through a hostile wilderness to the homeland promised since the time of Abraham, and forged bonds between the people and Yahweh that would last for more than 3,000 years. It is a great story, beautifully told in the books of Exodus, Numbers, and Deuteronomy.

I once climbed for thirty brutal minutes under the blazing sun to reach the top of the great pyramid of Cheops. Bruised and sore from having scuffed against massive sandstone blocks, gulping for air, I finally stood atop the pyramid 450 feet above the Giza plain. To the East, green loops of the Nile snaked across the desert, and beside the river sat Cairo in a blue haze. Southward, lesser pyramids marched along the bluffs like toy figures. To the West, only sand. That was the Egypt that Moses knew, not the squarish land on today's map, just a strip of green lining the Nile for 600 miles.

The river draws scarcely a drop of rain from the bright skies; it has no tributary in Egypt to bring it water. The burning sun and the thirsty sand drink its moisture. Yet people settled in this valley thousands of years ago. When grasslands withered on the plateaus and game became scarce, the Nile's surging summer floods enriched Egypt's soil with layer upon layer of silt from the heart of Africa.

That is why the Israelites came there, and it is why others have been drawn there from time to time out of famine. Egypt was the bread basket of the world. A vibrant nation flourished here early on, the riches of its soil buttressed by gold and copper from nearby mountains.

Slaves filled Egypt's kitchens and weaving rooms, swelled her armies, and worked on her shrines. One pharaoh boasted of carrying off 232 Asian princesses, 323 princesses, and 270 court women in one campaign, and 89,000 warriors in another. Nile-based ships ventured to Crete and Phoenicia and southward to the land of Punt for incense, myrrh, gum, and ivory.

During the early dynasties great pyramids arose, wonders of the world and symbols of the yearning for immortality and of the power, skill, and organization of the Egyptian state under its kings. But even Egypt had its ups and downs. Even the pharaohs were confronted by persons as powerful as they were in skill and power. And what we will see in our story is a standoff (and finally a victory) between Pharaoh Ramses II, one of the mightiest Egypt ever produced, and Moses, the shepherd of Yahweh.

For almost two hours I rode north out of Cairo in an old Chevrolet driven by an Egyptian pastor. We were headed to Tanta and on into the delta of the Nile, to the very land of Goshen, where Moses was born. This is where Joseph's brothers came with their families and flocks to dwell in time of famine. In this land the Bible calls Goshen, they prospered until, "there rose up a new king who knew not Joseph." And fearful lest the aliens in his borderlands might join his enemies, this pharaoh ordered every son born to the Israelites to be cast into the river. But one of these sons, saved ironically by pharaoh's daughter, was Moses.

From what the Bible calls "bulrushes," Moses was pulled out by pharaoh's daughter. His own mother was selected as his nurse and he was raised in pharaoh's court. But despite his nurture in pharaoh's court, Moses continued to identify with his Israelite kinsmen, as is vividly described in a scene in which he looses his temper with an Egyptian taskmaster. The taskmaster was beating and Israelite slave and Moses killed him. Then fearing that his act of murder would reach the ear of the king, he flees into the land of Midian, across the Red Sea.

There, after a romance that began at a well, he married the daughter of Jethro. Here is a portion of the story from the book of Exodus:

> Moses was looking after the flock of Jethro, his father-in-law, priest of Midian. He led his flock to the far side of the wilderness and came to Horeb, the mountain of God. There the angel of Yahweh appeared to him in the shape of a fire, coming from the middle of a bush. Moses looked; there was the bush blazing but it was not being burnt up. "I must go and look at this strange sight," Moses said "and see why the bush is not burnt." Now Yahweh saw him go forward to look, and God called to him from the middle of the bush. "Moses, Moses!" he said. "Here I am" he answered. "Come no nearer" he said. "Take off your shoes, for the place on which you stand is holy ground. I am the God of your father, the God of Abraham, the God of Isaac, and the God of Jacob." At this Moses covered his face, afraid to look at God.
>
> And Yahweh said, "I have seen the miserable state of my people in Egypt. I have heard their appeal to be free of their slave-drivers. Yes, I am well aware of their sufferings. I mean to deliver them out of the hands of the Egyptians and bring them up out of that land to a land

rich and broad, a land where milk and honey
flow. . . . And now the cry of the sons of
Israel has come to me, and I have witnessed the
way in which the Egyptians oppress them, so
come, I send you to Pharaoh to bring the sons
of Israel, my people, out of Egypt." [1]

This story of Moses' discovery of Yahweh is one of the master-
pieces of the Old Testament. It must be read with religious imagination
and empathy, and it must be read as poetry, for it communicates a
dimension of meaning that cannot be cramped into the limits of precise
prose. It would be foolish, for instance, to rationalize the burning bush
as though this vision were something that could have been seen with the
objective eye of a camera.

Fire is frequently the symbol for the manifestation of God in the
Old Testament; whatever Moses saw was transformed into a religious
sign of the divine presence. Moses' vision awakened the reality and the
realization that he was truly standing on holy ground; at that moment and
on that mountain rendezvous he was met by God.

At first, like any one of us, Moses would have wondered how
the bush could burn without being consumed. But in the story, attention
shifts quickly from seeing the bush to hearing God speak. That's the
important thing. The conversation shows how real the slavery of the
Jews in Egypt had been in the mind of Moses. Remember, he ran away
from Egypt after an indignant outburst of anger against the slave driver.
Thus, when Yahweh speaks to Moses, he speaks of something real in
Moses' life, and his speech is a declaration of what he, Yahweh, plans to
do. Notice how several verbs are used to describe Yahweh's intention:
He has *seen* the affliction of the people; he has *heard* their cry; Yahweh
knows their sufferings, and has *come down* to deliver them.

Yahweh is not aloof from the human scene of oppression; he
takes part in human affairs to work out his purpose. He makes himself
known by his deeds, which are historic events. Right here we come to
the very heart of Israel's historic faith; right here we come to the heart of

---

[1] *Exodus* 3:1-10.

what is truly unique in our Judaic-Christian tradition. God is not a mystic; God is not remote. God is immediate; God cares.

From this point on, Moses is the very manifestation of Yahweh. He goes to Pharaoh, moves to the very center of the court, confronts the mighty king of all Egypt, and in the name of Yahweh says, "Let my people go." For all time he states the fact that oppression, enslavement, and denial of human rights is alien to the purpose of Yahweh for his people. And after the event of the Passover, they did go, through the sea which parted before them and closed upon the Egyptians. Miriam and others danced and sang in celebration before the Lord.

They then went to the holy mountain at Sinai to receive the law, and afterwards they wandered in the wilderness where they were forged into an effective, cohesive unit.

But what happened at the burning bush was the most amazing thing in the whole story. From that point on a new concept is understood by Moses about this Yahweh. This was not a god like other gods. This Yahweh cared about the people and involved himself in securing justice and freedom. The temptation of the Church is to try to force this Yahweh back into conventional modes, but the stories of Israel and the Church's own memory will not have it so. For the primal disclosure of the Bible is that Yahweh makes a move toward earth to identify with his people, responding to the groans of an oppressed people. It's an irreversible move, a decisive move. The evidence of Scripture, of the prophets, and of the true saints of the Church is that they continue to witness for and to this discernment of God, and always against the temptation to drive Yahweh back to Heaven, to squeeze Yahweh back into the safety and serenity and irrelevance of other gods. That is still the decisive battle in the Church.

This Yahweh, whom Moses discovers, is the one who intends to have solidarity with his people. Yahweh makes no other claim, no special exemption for himself. What a God!

> He was despised and rejected by men and
> women, acquainted with grief, as one from

whom they hid their faces. He was despised
and we esteemed him not.[2]

This God bears none of the marks of a god. This Yahweh has
given up power in the certainty that real saving power is found in uncom-
promising faithfulness toward the oppressed, the very posture that other
gods in heaven cannot countenance. Perhaps it is too familiar to us, so
familiar that we now mistake how subversive this covenant made by
Yahweh really is. This solidarity with the oppressed on the part of
Yahweh shows that such solidarity is possible, even expected, on earth!
There will be no community on earth so long as we rally around the old
god-claims of self-sufficiency and omnipotence, because self-sufficient,
omnipotent, isolated and impassive people are incapable of being in
community or embracing solidarity. That is what is behind the words of
Jesus when he said, "The cup poured out for you is the new covenant in
my blood." It means that whenever we eat the bread and drink the cup
at communion, we engage in a subversive minority report.

Precisely because of being broken and poured out, this bread
and wine will never be fully accommodated to the interest of the old age,
for that age wants the bread unbroken and the wine still filling the cup.
The world yearns for gods who do not take risks, but that is not the
Yahweh whom Moses discovered.

What was Moses like then? He was a man of very human traits
whose anger was not glossed over in the record. But he was also a great
prophet. Long afterward it was remembered that, "By a prophet the
Lord brought Israel from Egypt."

Moses had a concern for human justice; he liberated people and
led them with a knowledge of this unique God. Pharaoh, his adversary,
is not remembered. Before Moses died he dictated what should be put
on his memorial, "King of Kings am I. If anyone would know how great
I am, and where I lie, let him surpass one of my works." But it was not
to be. The poet Shelley took this up and wrote:

---

[2] *Isaiah* 53: 2-3.

I met a traveller from an antique land
Who said: Two vast and trunkless legs of stone
Stand in the desert. . . . Near them, on the sand
Half sunk, a shattered visage lies, whose frown,
And wrinkled lip and sneer of cold command,
Tell that its sculptor well those passions read
Which yet survive, stamped on these lifeless things,
The hand that mocked them, and the heart that fed:
And on the pedestal these words appear:
"My name is Ozymandias, king of kings:
Look on my works, ye mighty, and despair!"
Nothing beside remains. Round the decay
Of that colossal wreck, boundless and bare
The lone and level sands stretch far away.[3]

The description is true, for in that temple today lie the shattered pieces of the fallen colossus of Ramses II. But Moses has a growing influence in the world; the passion for justice and the powerful faith which he embodied and stamped on a few thousand half-nomads more than three millennia ago continues to grow in the world.

He was slow of speech, they wrote of him, but he rose to a challenge of faith and became a fighter grappling with mighty Pharaoh and prevailing. He bore of his people in his bosom; he was a provider, an intercessor, humble, selfless, never resting, never giving up.

*   *   *   *   *

The story of Moses is found in the books of *Exodus*, *Leviticus*, *Numbers* and *Deuteronomy*. There are two main sources of the material in these books which were interwoven in later years.

---

[3] Percy Bysshe Shelley, "Ozymandius," *New Oxford Book of English Verse, 1250-1950* (Helen Gardner, editor), Oxford University Press, 1972.

Chapter Six

THE SCARLET THREAD

The struggle for land has always been one of the most powerful drives in any national history. Here in the USA we know that. In story and song we rehearse the stirring epic of immigrants who landed on the Atlantic seaboard and eventually pushed the frontier all the way to the Pacific at great cost and hardship, often with fierce warfare. But, as someone said, "early settlers fell on their knees, then on the aborigines." Unfortunately such men and women are still with us in some number, affirming that the hand of God guided the destiny of the new nation, despite the sordid record of injustice and violence. We have quotes from some of the leaders and long passages in school textbooks from the 1800s that claim that God led us to slaughter and rob in the name of civilization and progress.

Move now in your mind almost halfway around the world and 4,000 years back in time to the Fertile Crescent. That strategic crescent of land starts in Egypt with the Nile Valley, goes narrowly up the eastern end of the Mediterranean, then curves eastward and downward to follow the Tigris and Euphrates Valley to the Persian Gulf. It was the scene of fierce and constant struggle for land, and it was used as a highway by people from Arabia, Asia Minor, the Caucasian highland, and Egypt. All sought a strip of the good earth to call their own.

Into this dynamic arena came the Hebrews. Like many others in the ancient world they were at first a landless people. They belonged to the floating population, the unsettled elements of society. They were wanderers seeking a land in order to settle down, participate in a society, and fulfill their historical destiny. Their struggle to obtain land entailed much suffering and the slaughter of many Canaanite natives. But it was their firm conviction that Yahweh, their God, was with them in the rough and tumble of the conflict. Here is the ancient liturgy preserved in the book called Deuteronomy:

My father was a wondering Aramaean. he
went down into Egypt to find refuge there, few
in numbers; but there he became a nation,
great, mighty, and strong. The Egyptians ill-
treated us, they gave us no peace and inflicted
harsh slavery on us. But we called on Yahweh
the God of our fathers. Yahweh heard our
voice and saw our misery, our toil and our
oppression; and yahweh brought us out of Egypt
with mighty hand and outstretched arm, with
great terror, and with signs and wonders. he
brought us here and gave us this land, a land
where milk and honey flow. [1]

That was the dream, a land of milk and honey. An Arab-Christ-
ian friend of mine once drove me from Jerusalem to Jericho. It is a
quick trip down a winding road through the barren, brown and seemingly
lifeless hills east of Jerusalem. He was pointing all that out, as he drove,
and he asked me, "Do you know why Moses died over there on Mt. Nebo
before he could come into the land of milk and honey?" I began to give
the usual biblical answer but was interrupted. "I'll tell you why," he said,
"Moses promised them a land of milk and honey and they followed him
through the desert to get to it. Then he got up there on the mountain,
took one look at the land, and died of a heart attack." But to wanderers
who were used to life in a barren wilderness, Canaan was a veritable
paradise.

But Yahweh your God is bringing you into a
prosperous land, a land of streams and springs,
of waters that well up from the deep in valleys
and hills, a land of wheat and barley, of vines,
of figs, of pomegranates, a land of olives, of oil,
of honey, a land where you will eat bread

---

[1] *Deuteronomy* 26:5-10.

without stint, where you will want nothing, a
land where the stones are of iron, where the
hills may be quarried for copper. You will eat
and have all you want and you will bless
Yahweh your God in the rich land he has given
you. [2]

It was not an easy journey, it took a long time and many died on
the way. The prophets would not let the people forget those days of
hardship by their mothers and fathers in the faith. They would gather
the people on a hillside and recite the history, it would sound something
like this:

In ancient days your ancestors lived beyond
the river like Terah, the father of Abraham, and
they served other gods. Then Yahweh bright
your father Abraham and your mother Sarah
from beyond the river and led them through the
land to Canaan. Yahweh increased their
descendants and gave them Isaac. To Isaac and
Rebekah he gave Jacob and Esau. To Esau he
gave the mountain country of Seir as his possession. Jacob and Rachael and their sons and
daughters were set down into Egypt. Then
Yahweh sent Moses and Aaron and Miriam
and plagued Egypt with mighty wonders. And
they brought the people out of it. Yahweh
brought our people out of Egypt and they came
to the sea, and the Egyptians pursued your
ancestors with chariots and horsemen. They
called on Yahweh and he spread a thick fog
between them and the Egyptians and made the
sea go back on them and over them. They saw
with their own eyes the things Yahweh did in

---

[2] *Deuteronomy* 8:7-10.

Egypt. Then for a long time the people lived in
the wilderness until Yahweh brought them into
the land of the Amorites who lived beyond the
Jordan. They made war on your ancestors but
Yahweh gave them into your hands.

Then Moses, our leader died, and the voice
of Yahweh said to Joshua, "Moses my servant
is dead, rise, it is time, and cross the Jordan
here you and all this people with you. As I was
with Moses, so I will be with you. Be strong
and of a good courage. Be not afraid, neither
be you dismayed, for the Lord your God is with
you whithersoever you go." [3]

So Joshua, intrepid general and brilliant military strategist,
started the great conquest of Canaan, a land about the size and shape of
the state of Vermont. He waged war against fierce barbaric kings with
stubborn armies, and the strife lasted many years.

Joshua's first move was to march from Moab, where Moses had
died, down the valley to the Jordan River. They were not far from the
vanished foundations of Sodom and Gomorrah, those wicked cities that
Abraham had dealt with, and all about them lay volcanic dust, desolation,
and pillars of salt. This barren land is far below sea level and the heat is
intense, but they moved on to a higher, better, well-populated land. Near
Jericho they found a civilization already quite old. Jericho was the key
fortification for the whole lower valley. Joshua wondered how big it was,
how many defenders it had, how thick the walls were, and what provisions the city had against siege. Joshua needed information to plan his
attack, and so he sent two of his most trusted men into the city dressed
as travelers. It is easy to imagine these two young men from the desert
walking through the gates of Jericho, anxious to avoid notice. The walls
represented the city's greatest strength, and the army of Joshua could not
move inside until they were breached or destroyed.

---

[3] *Joshua* 1:1-5.

We know from archeological studies that Jericho, like many other cities in those days, really had two walls with a gap of eight to twelve feet between them. Houses were sometimes built literally in the walls and over the walls, with windows that looked out beyond the city. Such a house is the setting for this Bible story.

It is the story of a woman named Rahab. Like the longer story of another famous non-Israelite woman named Ruth, it belongs to a large collection of historical tales that were deeply loved and often retold in the life of Israel.

Rahab's house was between the walls and had windows that looked out through the wall. It was a house, not a home, for Rahab was a harlot, actually a madam. City authorities must frequently have seen unfamiliar characters go in and out of her house, and so it would not be unusual for two strangers like the ones in our story to be seen entering it.

I wonder about that encounter. These two young men had certainly never before met such a person as Rahab! They had been born to desert wandering and had grown hard from that spartan life. Here before them was a woman with a painted face, red lips, jewelry, silken robes, perfume, and the jingle of bracelets and bangle of beads.

She received them and gave them lodging, and their choice of a stopping place is not so strange. Where better to get information? As a matter of fact the visit to Rahab's house was the sum total of their reconnaissance activity.

Somehow the king of Jericho learned the spies were there, sent in his FBI and demanded that Rahab surrender them, for, he said, "they have come to spy out the land." Before the agents of the king arrived (how did she know they were coming?), Rahab hid Joshua's spies on the flat roof of her house under great bundles of flax placed there for drying. Then she told the king's agents: "Yet two strangers did come. I didn't know who they were or what they wanted." After all, they were just a couple of patrons from whom it was not customary to require credentials. Who uses a credit card in a house like that?

She told the agents that the men left under cover of night, "Why don't you try to catch them up the valley?" So off went the agents of the king while Joshua's spies hid safely on the roof.

Why did she lie? Had she or one of her ladies overheard conversation that the soldiers and citizens of Jericho were not sure that they could withstand an attack? Had she heard about the strength of the approaching Israelites? For whatever reasons, Rahab lied to the king's men and came to terms with the spies. She was convinced that the city would fall, and she made a deal. "Kindness is a two way street," she said, "I've sheltered you, you shelter me. Protect me and my family." "Fair enough," they said, "but what sign shall we use so that the army of Joshua will know of the covenant and not destroy you?" One of the spies plucked a scarlet thread from among the material ready to be made into garments, "Hang this in your window," he said. Then Rahab let Joshua's spies down from a window in the wall by a rope, and they returned safely to Joshua with the information about Jericho.

When Joshua and his men crossed the Jordan and arrived at Jericho, the city had been barricaded; no one came out, no one went in. Joshua formed his troops, put the priests carrying the sacred Ark in front, and began a march around the walls. They blew trumpets and showed off the Ark, the symbol of the might and power of Yahweh. For six days they marched in that way. The seventh day began as on the previous six, and by this time it must have been like the sixth re-run of a TV show. The guards on the wall yawned with boredom, and the people of Jericho went about their business; they had seen enough of this foolishness.

That is just what Joshua wanted. Suddenly he sounded the rams horn; his troops yelled at the top of their lungs and attacked, and the defense collapsed!

Rahab and her family were taken outside the city and saved, and from that time on Rahab has had a special fascination for the people of Israel. There are several things we should note about her. First she had a deep concern for her family. It was not a case of "save me," it was "save my family." Second, tradition has it that Rahab eventually married Joshua, and we do know that Rahab's family was received into Israel. Third, there is another tradition that Rahab was the ancestress of eight prophets and priests, including Jeremiah. Most astonishing of all, in the genealogy of Jesus in Matthew's gospel, we find the name of Rahab along with the name of three other women; Ruth, Tamar, and Bathesheba.

Fourth, in the book of Hebrews in the New Testament, Rahab is named among the heroes and heroines of the faith, while Joshua is passed over. Finally, in the New Testament book of James, Rahab is used as an illustration of a person who lived by faith, and the only other Old Testament character mentioned is Abraham.

Unless Rahab had faith, she would never have taken the risk against all common knowledge of identifying her future with the fortunes of Israel. It was a chance in a million that these nomads from the desert, without artillery, chariots or siege machines would conquer Jericho.

Unless Rahab had been prepared to risk all to help the spies, her faith would have been a useless thing. So we learn, from this very human story, that faith and deeds are not opposites but inseparables. No person will ever be moved to action without faith, and no person's faith is real until it moves the person to action.

But back to Joshua for a moment. He went on to conquer Canaan for the tribes of Israel, and he parceled out the land from Dan to Ber-sheba. For a closing scene, he called all Israel together for a great assembly at Schechem and placed before them this challenge:

> So now, fear Yahweh and serve him perfectly and sincerely. Put away the gods that your ancestors served beyond the River and in Egypt, and serve Yahweh. But if you will not serve Yahweh, choose today whom you wish to serve, Yahweh, or the gods of the Amorites in whose land you are now living. As for me and my house, we will serve Yahweh. [4]

So the beat went on, yielding a gradual understanding of their Yahweh and a progressive revelation of yahweh's nature. A voice from a burning bush; a cloudy pillar; manna and quails in the desert; the law from a mountainside; a king called David; and the prophets Amos, Jeremiah, and Hosea are all part of this history. And finally came a man

---

[4] *Joshua* 24:14-15.

called Jesus, who most crisply of all reflected a God called Yahweh and a way of life called love.

*   *   *   *   *

The story of Rahab is found in *Joshua*, chapter 2.

Chapter Seven

THE PROBLEM WITH LONG HAIR

One of the most beautiful things about our faith is the way our mothers and fathers preserved stories of all kinds. You name it, you can find love ballads, folk tales, mysteries, and accounts of patriotic heros and heroines, all in the Bible. This chapter illustrates that, since it is really a collection of very short stories about a hero named Samson who was one of the Judges of Israel.

Our faith-history begins way back in 1725 B.C. when Abraham and Sarah left Ur of the Chaldees and made their 1,000 mile walk to the new country that they called Canaan. Canaan was already populated with people at that time, and Sarah and Abraham and their relatives had some difficulty finding places to graze their flocks and settle down.

The fragile land led their grandchildren to Egypt where they lived for several centuries. Most of the time in Egypt was a period of prosperity for them, and they enjoyed their stay. But then a "Pharaoh who knew not Joseph" took power and enslaved the people of Israel.

They were led on a memorable Exodus out of oppression in Egypt by Moses and Miriam. After a period of wandering in the Sinai wilderness, they crossed to the west side of the Jordan River, conquered Jericho under the leadership of Joshua, and eventually subdued most of the countryside except the costal plain along the Mediterranean.

But two problems remained. One was how the people of Israel were to exist intermingled with the original inhabitants of Canaan. It now seems clear , that there was slow assimilation and intermarriage instead of one large conquest or battle that would have cleared out the people who originally resided there and left the place free for the tribes of Israel. There clearly were some wars and exterminations, but pockets of resistance remained long after the "conquest."

The second problem was religious. The Israelites had brought with them a monotheistic and imageless worship of a high moral level.

Their life had been that of pastoral desert nomads not directly dependent upon the fertility of the soil and with no need for agricultural festivals associated with seed time and harvest. The Canaanites, on the other hand, were an agricultural people, whose religion was bound up with sustaining the fertility of the soil and the cycle of nature. They had many deities. So, as they came into Canaan, the leaders of our faith-family, were faced with the problem of keeping their religion pure.

Both of these problems were faced by the establishment of Judges. The Judges were strong men and women from all different tribes whom we would call "local war-lords." They had enough charisma and power to raise an army and do well in fighting for country and religion. Some fourteen Judges are mentioned in the biblical book by that name, but we hear most about Deborah, Gideon and Samson.

This story began with a familiar note of a couple that is childless; Sarah and Abraham had been concerned because they were pledged to be parents of a great nation, but had no children. Sarah laughed when some strangers who were messengers of Yahweh declared that she would have a son when she was in her nineties. Of course, she did have a son, and so we got to this point in the history of our faith-family.

Well, this story is that a of a couple from the tribe of Dan who had no children. An angel of Yahweh appeared to the woman and said,

> You are barren and have had no child. But from now on take great care. Take no wine or strong drink, and eat nothing unclean. For you will conceive and bear a son. No razor is to touch his head, for the boy shall be God's nazarite from the time of your womb. It is he who will begin to rescue Israel from the power of the Philistines. [1]

So from the beginning, Samson had been dedicated to be a nazarite, a group of specially dedicated persons who would drink no wine (before or after its time) nor cut their hair, nor shave their faces.

---

[1] *Judges* 13:3-5.

But notice that the Nazarites were not teetotalers on moral grounds; wine was a characteristic product of agricultural civilization and well-trimmed hair and beards were the mark of city dwellers. Thus, the nazarite movement was really a protest against the new life centered on field and town in the name of the old dessert tradition.

Samson was committed to this Nazarite life from his birth, but he consciously broke all the vows that his parents had made, going so far as to marry a Philistine woman.

But let me tell the story in sequence. It is a fascinating one, well written with all the drama that a good storyteller from the Middle East can put into it.

Samson's youth is passed over and we next meet him falling in love with, as I said, a Philistine. Now Philistines were the ones I spoke of before who inhabited the coast from Gaza to Mt. Carmel. Apparently there was a peace at the moment. Since there were no sharp lines drawn between the tribes and countries, no passports or visas were necessary and Samson found himself in a Philistine town where he became enamored of a beautiful young woman. He hurried home and demanded that his parents get her for him.

His mother said, "Why must you break your mothers heart? Is there no woman among those of your own clan or among your whole nation for you to seek as a wife instead you go outside for a Philistine? Why can't you find a nice Jewish girl?"

But Samson was adamant, and so, like the spoiled son he was, he got his way. Samson took his parents to Timnah and pointed out the girl. They made arrangements and a date was set for the wedding.

On their way to Timnah, Samson was attracted by the growl of a lion. He was possessed by abnormal strength, and he literally tore the lion apart by shear brute force and left the carcass by the roadside. Sometime later, as he returned for the marriage service, he found that the empty carcass of the lion had been filled with honeycomb by a swarm of bees. He stopped and took honey out of the carcass of the lion to eat.

Finally Samson arrived for the wedding. As a preliminary, he entertained the young men of the village at a feast. The thirty young Philistines who attended probably did not think much of this Israelite who was about to take away one of the beauties of the town. When music and dancing girls failed to raise the gloom, Samson told his guests that he had a riddle for them. Then he said, "if you find the answer to my riddle within the seven days of this feast, I will give you each a new set of clothes. And if you fail, you shall give me thirty new suits."

"Ask your riddle," they said, "we're listening!"

So, Samson said,

> Out of the eater, came what is eaten
> And out of the strong, came what is
> sweet.

Three days went by and they couldn't solve Samson's riddle. The wager involved a considerable amount of clothing which neither side could afford to loose. On the fourth day, unable to solve the riddle, the Philistines put pressure on Samson's wife to discover the answer. When they threatened to burn down her father's house, Samson's new wife turned on the strongest power known, her tears, to persuade Samson to tell his secret.

Samson said he hadn't even told his parents, so why should he tell her. She said, "If you love me, you'll tell me your secret." And at last, worn out by her pleading, Samson told her the solution to the riddle, unaware of either the threat to her or her intended treachery.

When the young men came up with the answer to the riddle at the very last moment, Samson's rage knew no bounds. He answered them in a jingle with the same form as the riddle:

> If you had not plowed with my heifer,
> You would not have found out my riddle.

Samson didn't have thirty suits of clothes with which to pay his wager, and in his rage he solved his problem by killing thirty other Philistines and giving their clothes to the banqueters. After all, he had not said that they would be new suits! In any event, the final feasting of the wedding week was scarcely over when Samson, still in a rage, deserted his wife. Her father had already received Samson's gift in exchange for the girl, and he saw a chance to make a further profit. He immediately gave her to Samson's best man!

When Samson's anger had cooled, he decided to return to his wife and discovered that she had been given to another man. He became very angry, and embarked on a vendetta which showed that he was cunning as well as strong.

Samson captured 300 foxes, tied them in pairs by their tails and fastened a burning torch to each pair. He then set them loose in the wheat fields of the Philistines, burning their grain and also their olive orchards.

Naturally the Philistines went after Samson. But when the had captured him, he broke the ropes with which he was bound and killed a large number of them with the jawbone of an ass.

The second woman to get Samson into trouble was a harlot from Gaza, the southernmost of the Philistine cities. He really did have an attraction to Philistine women!

When the Philistines discovered that he had come to visit this second woman, they set out to grab him as he left the city. They figured that would be in the morning, because the gates would be closed for the night preventing him from leaving under cover of darkness. But Samson stole the gate itself and carried it to Hebron some thirty-eight miles away.

Finally Samson became interested in a woman closer to home. Deliah was her name, but the intrigue still remained. The Philistine rulers offered Deliah a fabulous sum if she would discover the secret of her lovers strength. Deliah was willing to try and started out by saying something like: "O Sammy dear, what makes you such a big he-man? How did you get such wonderful muscles? How will your loving little Deliah ever make you behave?"

Samson decided to have some fun with her and suggested that if he were bound with seven fresh bow strings she could control him.

Well, she followed his suggestions and bound him then cried, "The Philistines are here," but he laughed and snapped the bow strings and the Philistines disappeared. They repeated the stunt with new ropes which snapped like threads.

Samson knew that his strength lay in his long hair. He was really enjoying his little joke with Deliah, so he thought he would see how close he could come to telling the truth and still play with her. Seeing Deliah's weaving loom, Samson suggested that if his hair were woven into a rug he would be helpless. So, Deliah got him to sleep, wove his hair into a web of the loom, and made it tight with a pin. She discovered that wasn't going to work either only after the Philistines came roaring in and Samson had ripped the whole loom apart.

But Deliah eventually got her lover to tell her about his hair. Maybe she made him drunk, or drugged his food, we don't know. But she got him to sleep and had a barber shave off his hair.

When he awoke and discovered his long hair was gone, he was ashamed and disgusted with himself. This time the Philistines came in and successfully captured him. They put out his eyes and took him to Gaza, where he had stolen the city gates. There he was hitched to a mill stone in place of a donkey and made to grind grain. But, as the story goes, "the hair that had been shorn off began to grow again."

The Philistines were finally happy; they had disgraced the man who had so often made a laughing stock of them. At one of their great religious feasts they demanded that the giant be put on exhibition so that they might make further fun of him. He was lead in by a boy. The temple was full, and a great crowd had gathered to see this rascal of whom they had heard so much. Considerable time had elapsed since his capture, for Samson's hair had grown in again.

He was set between two pillars that supported the temple roof. Summoning all his strength, he gave a mighty shove against the pillars, and the temple caved in on Samson and the Philistines. As the roof came down, Samson cried out: "May I die with the Philistines." And he did. The building fell on the chief rulers and all the people there.

The book of Judges says, "Those he killed in his death, outnumbered those he had killed in his life." His brothers and his whole family came down and carried him to the tomb of his father.

I don't know why I can't just leave this story of a Jewish folk hero right here, but Presbyterian ministers just can't do that. Let me take a few minutes to give you my reflections on this story.

I see here a lesson about undisciplined power. Both this ancient giant and the great nations of our day face the same temptations and the same need for restraints. Possessed of power greater than at any previous time in history, and having discovered and released an energy force too vast for us to really understand or control, I wonder if we have any higher concept of what power is than did this ancient Israelite?

Samson didn't know what to do with his power. He didn't know how to employ it creatively, and he let it get the best of him. We need deliverance from the perils of the power that we have. The story that has been told time and again in the last decade of nuclear proliferation is a sobering one. We thought that as "good people" we should be the only ones to have the bomb. But then the Soviet Union made one, and France exploded theirs, and on it went, until now even impoverished India has the bomb!

Everyone talked about peace and said the bomb was an instrument for keeping the peace. Each nation said they could control it. But, the question now becomes, who are the "good people" and who are the "bad people" that have this awesome weapon? They all have the lives of the world in their hands. To understand and deal with this kind of power is even more important in our day than it was in Samson's. Today we have the power to destroy all the cities of the Soviet Union many times over. We have the power to obliterate the world, to return it to the chaos out of which it began. We have stockpiled the equivalent of over twenty-five tons of TNT for every man, woman and child in the planet. Let me tell you it doesn't take anyway near twenty-five tons of TNT to do away with Bill Phillippe. Somehow we need to be reminded, that power is always a means and must never be an end. When it is regarded as an end in itself, it is useless and dangerous and leads to futility and chaos. But, how easily it can become an end. Capricious power is the danger in our world today, above all others. The USA and the Soviet Union square off and look like adolescents using their strength to tie the tales of foxes together with fire brands to send them through the fields, or to steal the gates of Gaza. The tragedy of Samson's life was that he used his power for unworthy ends. Even knowing that his strength came from God, he used it for destruction, he used it for lust, and he used it for revenge. Will we have no wiser use for our own power than to push with blind and senseless pressures against the columns which uphold our society?

The death of this giant of Israel reminds us of the perils of the strength of persons, and of nations. It is perilous unless it is mellowed and humbled and controlled by the direction of a wise and loving God whose aim is peace and whose goal is shalom, the fullest possible sustainable life for every person, everywhere.

*   *   *   *   *

The story of Samson is told in *Judges*, Chapters 13-16.

Chapter Eight

THE PROBLEM WITH LOST ASSES

Yesterday, along with getting a good case of sunburn and some heartburn, we celebrated the 111th anniversary of our founding as a nation. I thought it would be interesting therefore, to reflect upon the founding of the nation of Israel, or at least of its monarchy.

It's a terribly familiar story, because, you see, the problem was the cost. Over the past few years we've heard a great deal about the cost of government in the United States, and everyone knows that the way to keep something from costing too much, is not to start it at all. Once you get the thing going, it's very difficult to keep it under control and almost impossible to hack it back in size. Well that's what Samuel and Yahweh told the people of their day. Here's how the story goes.

Up until the time of our story, the people of Israel had been governed by Judges, local warlords who kept peace both between the tribes and with neighboring nations. But the people had increased in numbers and their needs had changed as they settled down into an agricultural mode of existence. Then they came face to face with a more formidable enemy, the Philistines. The Philistines were a fragment of a sea-going people, inhabitants of the coasts of Asia Minor and of the Agean Islands who had been driven out by a great migration of Aryan peoples. The Trojan War was one part of this displacement. Having been repelled from settling in Egypt by Ramsees III, the Philistines had settled on the coastal planes of Israel from present day Gaza to Mt. Carmel. Though of a totally different culture than the Israelites, they quickly adopted the language and customs of their neighbors.

On the coastal plane they were grouped in five cities, each with its own ruler or king, but they often acted together. Soon they began to press up from the costal planes into the hills, and there they clashed with the Israelites. The struggle proved unequal.

The Philistines were superior in culture and military art to the Israelites, and they had in their number many "giants" whose physical stature rendered them formidable in hand to hand combat. The Philistines first overcame the nearby cities of Judah and Dan. Then they pushed on to establish their mastery over the territory of Ephram and Benjamin, making the inhabitants of those cities into slaves. They had garrisons stationed at important posts to keep down their subjects, and they took strong measures to disarm the population, even forbidding the Israelites to have blacksmiths and compelling them to go to Philistia to get farm tools sharpened.

If a Judge had now arisen and summoned the people to resist as in the past, freedom might have been obtained, but no leader appeared. Legend has extolled the exploits of Sampson, but even legend can attribute to him nothing but personal power. He had no ability to lead others. And there was not another like Deborah who could call forth the slumbering energy of local chiefs. More serious, for a long time Israel had lacked religious leadership. With the exception of Deborah, no persons since the days of Joshua had stood forth in any commanding way to speak to the people in the name of Yahweh.

But then a woman named Hannah had a son who called Samuel, and onto the stage came the next great actor in the history of our faith. At the birth of Samuel, Hannah sang a song of rejoicing which must have influenced Mary, because many centuries later she sang a song very much like Hannah's at the birth of Jesus.

Hannah dedicated Samuel to God's service, and he was put in the hands of the prophet Eli for training. At fifteen years of age, Samuel became a guard of the Ark of Israel, sleeping in the same room where it was kept.

Old Eli's two sons, who were the best thing Israel had at that time for leadership, were botching things up pretty badly. In one battle against the Philistines they were convinced that if they had just taken the Ark of the Covenant with them, the Philistines would have been defeated. So they stole the Ark, without letting either Samuel or Eli know about it, for their next encounter.

The presence of the Ark in that battle greatly encouraged the Israelites and put fear into the hearts of the Philistines. But it made the

Philistines determined to fight all the harder lest they become slaves to the Israelites. Israel was defeated and the Ark was captured.

Scripture says Eli was a fat man, nearly a hundred years old; when he learned that the Ark had been captured, it was too much for him, and he fell backwards from his seat, broke his neck, and died. Eventually, the Ark was returned and Samuel became it's chief keeper. Not much is known about Samuel's life for about twenty years but it is clear that he becomes both a Judge and a national priest.

At this point in the story, having been dominated by the Philistines for over two decades, the people begin to clamor that they want a king like the Philistines or the Assyrians or others who were round about them. They wanted a king so that they too could control their own destiny, so that they would be free from foreign intervention.

"We want a king, we want a king," they all cried out.

Samuel said, " You have a king, Yahweh."

But the people said they wanted to see their king; they wanted to be like everyone else.

Up to this time, the Israelites had a very inexpensive form of government. Their God did not need a salary. Saul reminded them of this. He rehearsed their history from the time of the Exodus of Moses to the wilderness wanderings, to the conquering with Joshua, through the period of the Judges. "You've had it pretty good," he said, "and it hasn't cost you hardly a thing!" Listen to the story:

> All that Yahweh had said Samuel repeated to the people who were asking him for a king. He said, "These will be the rights of the king who is to reign over you. He will take your sons and assign them to his chariotry and cavalry, and they will run in front of his chariot. He will use them as leaders of a thousand and leaders of fifty; he will make them plough his ploughland and harvest his harvest and make his weapons of war and the gear for his chariots. He will also take your daughters as perfumers, cooks and bakers. He will take the best of your fields,

of your vineyards and olive groves and give them
to his officials. He will tithe your crops and
vineyards to provide for his eunuchs and his
officials. He will take the best of your
menservants and maidservants, of your cattle
and your donkeys, and make them work for
him. He will tithe your flocks, and you yourselves will become his slaves. When that day
comes, you will cry out on account of the king
you have chosen for yourselves, but on that day
God will not answer you.

The people refused to listen to the words of
Samuel. They said, "No! We want a king, so
that we in our turn can be like the other
nations; our king shall rule us and be our leader
and fight our battles." [1]

It's obvious from scripture that their were two major parties in
Israel, one pro-monarchy and the other anti-monarchy. Those who
wanted to establish a government with a King were cleaver enough to use
the Philistines as their reason to spend a lot of money on a King. (Does
that sound familiar? Every time someone wants to raise the defense
budget, we hear about Philistines who are about to get us.) If we don't
have a King the Philistines will get us! So a nation that had been built
upon the kingship of Yahweh, a nation that had discovered itself in the
hardness of the desert, a nation that had been dedicated to freedom sold
itself short and gave in to the scare-mongers and cries of fear.

I'm tempted to leave this sermon at this point to meditate as to
how our nation, born out of the ruggedness of freedom, succumbs so
easily again and again and again to the cries of fear. But, on with our
story.

The ninth chapter of this book introduces us to Samuel's choice
of a man named Saul from the tribe of Benjamin. Saul is out hunting
(actually, he is looking for his father's lost asses that had wandered

---

[1] *I Samuel* 8:10-20.

away). Saul hunted extensively, but with no success. He finally came to the town where Samuel was staying, and one of Saul's servants suggested that the priest might help them.

A sacrifice, with its accompanying feast, was about to be held, and, of course, Samuel was in charge. Believing that a special guest was going to arrive before the feast was over, he had the cooks set aside a choice portion. And along came Saul. Samuel knew in an instant that this was the one who would be King. So he said to him, "Forget about the lost asses, come to this banquet as my guest and spend the night." The choice portion of meat was given him (the leg and the tail), and a bed was spread on the rooftop to take advantage of the breeze.

Samuel knew Saul was the one. He was unusually tall, which would impress the Philistines; he was handsome, and he came from a well-to-do family. Doubtless they talked all night about the matter at hand. Then early in the morning, Samuel took a bottle of oil, poured it on Saul's head and told him he was to be King. Evidently, Saul was not terrible excited about all this. The story tells us that after the event he just went on home.

Samuel then called a gathering of all the tribes of Israel at Mt. Mizpah. There the people began to cast lots and do an elimination contest. Eleven tribes were eliminated, leaving the tribe of Benjamin. Then clans of the tribe of Benjamin were eliminated until only the clan of Matri remained. Then Samuel made the members of the clan of Matri come forward one at a time until the lot fell to Saul.

But Saul took off! They hunted for him and finally found him hiding among the baggage. That is the problem with lost asses; sometimes you go looking for them and find a responsibility that is far greater than you expect. That is what happened to Saul.

But Samuel did not desert Saul. He wrote a constitution for this new monarchy, and it was very clear that the King was *not* the supreme power. The King was to listen to the will of God, and the will of God would be interpreted through his prophets, like Samuel.

Saul tried to work under this new constitution, and he did well until the time he was told to go and exterminate a group of "sinners" in the city of Amalek. Saul decided to save the King, Agag, and the best of the sheep and the oxen, and to bring them back home with him. Samuel saw that as disobedience. What follows is a very bitter story, hard for us to understand perhaps, but a part of those early years of discovery of the relationship of the people to their God. For Samuel says:

> I regret having made you king, for you have
> turned away from me and have not carried out
> my orders. Since you have rejected the word of
> Yahweh, he has rejected you as king.[2]

As Samuel turned to go away, Saul caught at the hem of his garment and tore it. Samuel said to him,

> Today Yahweh has torn the kingdom of Israel
> form you and has given it to a neighbor of yours
> who is better than you.[3]

What bitter, rigid and inflexible words!   How far from the understanding of God we now know through Jesus.

If Samuel came no more to see Saul, what did he do? For a time he was inconsolable because he still loved Saul. Finally, by Yahweh's direction he had to go and anoint David to be the next King. But he did it reluctantly and he did it secretly. The next thing we know of is the recording of his death, "and all Israel gathered to lament him, and bury him in his house in Remah.[4]"

When Samuel died, Israel was on its way to a better future. All this leaves me with these thoughts to ponder:

> 1. That a nation founded on a strength and
> freedom should not make major decisions (or
> be bullied into making them) by cries of fear.

---

[2] *I Samuel* 12:10,23.

[3] *I Samuel* 12:28.

[4] *I Samuel* 25:1.

2. That a nation, no matter what its constitution or its dollar bills may say about trust in God, should be wary of those who simplistically believe that there are clean, neat answers to complex problems in an imperfect and pluralistic society.

A theocracy is *not* possible for us as a nation, any more than it proved suitable for ancient Israel. Despite the "moral majority's" claim, no one has a direct pipeline to God; we are all of us imperfect; we see and hear through a multitude of filters what we want to see and hear. But, 111 years have shown us that we *can* trust our God-given good sense as a collective and diverse people to strive for peace and liberty and justice for all.

*   *   *   *   *

The story of Saul is found in *I Samuel*, chapters 8-31.

Chapter Nine

SPIES AND COUNTERSPIES

W. C. Fields once said, "A man who doesn't like baseball, kids and dogs can't be all bad." This story is about a man who was an irreverent liar, a cheat, a swindler, an adulterer, and a murderer. But then, who's perfect? Can a guy like that be all bad?

This man also was sensitive, loyal, courageous, strong, and very bright. He was hated, loved, adored, and despised. He was a shepherd, a king, a poet, a warrior, a planner, a builder, and a diplomat. He was also an ancestor of Jesus called the Christ.

What sort of person could draw such a range of feelings? Only one who was free and confident, who lived with a lively knowledge of Yahweh, who developed a unique understanding of his limits and the expectations of yahweh to act in history. The person was David the great King of Israel.

This is the David who took another man's wife and made sure her husband was "in front of the battle to get killed." He is the man who wrote: "Have mercy upon me O Lord, for I have sinned against thee in thought and word and deed," and "The Lord is my shepherd, I shall not want. . . ."

There is no more romantic story to be found in world literature than that of the shepherd boy of Bethlehem who won a king's favor, then lost it and became a hunted outlaw, and then was made king himself; who took his people to a height never known before, but then sinned deeply and saw the implications work themselves out in his household until he died a heart-broken old man in the midst of the splendor he had created. No wonder the minstrels and storytellers of Israel delighted to tell of David.

His story begins about 1000 B.C.; David was keeping his father's sheep in the vicinity of Bethlehem. Tradition says he was the youngest of eight brothers, the grandson of Boaz and Ruth, and he is described as "red, a youth fair of eyes, good to look at."

Saul, the first King anointed by Samuel, had done badly. He had not followed yahweh, and had become a fear-ridden, haunted man. So Samuel was told to go find a new king. "How will I know," he asked, and Yahweh replied, "I'll tell you when you see him. Go."

Samuel set off and eventually found himself in Bethlehem looking over the sons of the family of Jessie. There he sees Eliab, tall, strong, and bold. Samuel thinks that he must surely be the one to be king, but Yahweh says, "I do not see as a man sees. Man looks at appearances, but Yahweh looks at the heart; this is not the one." And the same was true for one after another, until seven of Jessie's sons are rejected.

Finally, Samuel, in desperation, turns to Jessie and asks: "Are these all the sons you have?" And Jessie says, "There is still one left, the youngest, but he is out looking after the sheep." Samuel told Jessie to bring him in, and when Samuel saw him, Yahweh said to Samuel, "Come, anoint him, for this is the one."

But, it was not quite time to put David on the throne, so David continues to do his shepherd's tasks for some time. Finally David attracted the notice of King Saul. You have heard the story many times. This unknown boy, too young to be a soldier, visits his brothers at the front of a battle and hears the insolent challenge of a Philistine giant named Goliath. David offers to take up the challenge, and is brought before the king and clothed in Saul's own armor. But, David rejects the armor and instead takes his sling and rock (a device he had perfected while keeping wolves from the sheep) and struck down the Philistine, bringing victory to the Israelites.

Because of this event, Saul took David into his military service, and soon made him an officer over others. David's skill also brought him the friendship of Saul's son Jonathan.

So it was that David began a brilliant military career. He was the kind of man Saul had been gathering about him to form his shock troops, and the King gave him generous recognition. David won the friendship not only of Saul's son, but that of his daughter, Michael, as well, and in due course they were married.

David's fame continued to increase, and further exploits so expanded his popularity that it eclipsed that of Saul. At last, Saul could no longer endure the people regarding David as their charismatic hero. He feared that they would want to make David king, as well, and so he turned completely against David and tried repeatedly to kill him.

David fled and hid, but the King's suspicions were not allayed. It seemed to Saul that everyone was plotting against him, even his own son Jonathan and his closest advisors. When Saul heard that a family of Shiloh had unwittingly given aid to David in his flight, Saul had them butchered and their homes demolished. As for Michael, he took her back from David and gave her to another. Clearly, Saul was out of his mind.

Though David doubtless was ambitious, there is no evidence that he was actually plotting against Saul. But Saul was too fear-ridden to think clearly; his behavior damaged him irreparably and caused many to question his competence.

During this time, David fled to the wilds of his native Judah where his kinsmen, together with malcontents, fugitives, and distressed persons of all sorts, rallied around him. Out of this mob of desperadoes, a tough fighting force of some four hundred men soon emerged. For some time, David existed as a bandit chief, playing both ends against the middle, striking the Philistines as opportunity offered, and continually dodging Saul's clutches.

Saul continued to war against the Philistines and finally decided to engage them in a decisive battle. But, his strategy was poor, and he was motivated more by outrage than reason. The battle was lost, three of his sons were killed, and Saul killed himself.

With characteristic comprehension and alertness, David acted quickly; he went at once to Hebron, the largest city of Judah, where the people knew him as a strong leader and a seasoned soldier with a good reputation among his troops. There they acclaimed him King, as did the other tribes shortly after. The Philistines understood what was happening, but, before they could react, David had united the twelve tribes of Israel, struck, and won. That ended the Philistine threat.

David then turned his attention to the internal consolidation of his power. In a brilliant move, he selected a small town in the central highlands not claimed by any of the tribes, captured it, and made it his capital. He fortified it, built himself a royal house there, and, most important of all, brought the sacred Ark of Yahweh. The name of the town is Jerusalem. In one action he unified the state and centralized the worship of Yahweh in Jerusalem, beginning a tradition of feeling toward that city that has lasted to our day.

David went on to extend the boundaries of Israel. He defeated the Philistines, the Edomites, the Moabites, the Amonites and the Syrians. In a few short years he changed Israel from a disorganized group of tribes into a strong nation that controlled the trade route from Egypt to all the North and from the Phoenician seaports to the West. Under David, Israel was larger and stronger than at any other time.

But David sinned. He took Bathsheba, wife of Uriah, and then put Uriah in the front of a battle to get him killed. Solomon is born. Then the prophet Nathan fearlessly condemned David for his sin, and, though David repented, the seeds of his destruction were sown.

As the years passed, his children began plotting against him, especially Absalom. With ruthless ambition, Absalom plotted for four years before he broke forth in open revolt and had himself proclaimed King. The strength of his following was amazing. By his aloofness and inaction, David had lost much of his hold on the people, for recruits flocked to Absalom's side.

David was forced to flee for his life across the Jordan river, and the story of his flight is one of the saddest pictures in the Bible. We see the broken-hearted old king toiling up the Mount of Olives barefoot, his head covered, weeping as he goes. But David's resourcefulness did not forsake him altogether, and he left behind in Jerusalem his counsellor Hushai.

Hushai succeeded in preventing immediate pursuit of David, which would have done him in; Absalom delayed with fatal results. But, let Scripture itself tell the tale. Here is David by the Jordan river, weak and vulnerable. Absalom is triumphant for the moment, and he seeks advice from Ahithophel, a good military strategist. But then listen to Hushai, whom David had deliberately left behind. Listen and enjoy this story of Spies and Counterspies told 30 centuries ago!

Ahithophel said to Absalom, "Let me choose twelve thousand men and set off this very night in pursuit of David. I shall fall on him while he is tired and dispirited; I shall strike terror into him, and all the people who are with him will take flight. Then I shall strike down the king alone and bring all the people back to you, as a bride returns to her husband. You seek the life of only one man; the rest of the people will go unharmed." The suggestion appealed to Absalom and all the elders of Israel.

"Next call Hushai the Archite," Absalom said. "Let us hear what he too has to say." When Hushai came to Absalom, Absalom said, "This is what Ahithophel says. Are we to do as he suggests? If not, say something yourself." Hushai answered Absalom, "On this occasion the advice Ahithophel has offered is not good. You know," Hushai went on, "that your father and his men are champions and as angry as a wandering bear robbed of her cubs. Your father is used to warfare; he will not let the army rest during the night. At this very moment he is hiding in a hollow or somewhere else. If at the outset there are casualties among our troops, word will go round of disaster to the army supporting Absalom. And then even the valiant, with a heart like the heart of a lion, will be quite unmanned; for all Israel knows that your father is a champion and that the men with him are valiant. For my part, I offer this advice: Let all Israel, from Dan to Beersheba, muster round you, numerous as the sand on the seashore, with your royal person marching in their midst. We shall come up with him wherever he is to be found; we shall fall on him as

the dew falls on the ground, and not leave him
or one of the men with him alive. Should he
retire into a town, all Israel will brings ropes to
that town, and we will drag it into the wadi
until not a pebble of it is to be found." Then
Absalom and all the people of Israel sid, "The
advice of Hushai the Archite is better than the
advice of Ahithophel." Yahweh had determined
to thwart Ahithophel's shrewd advice and so to
bring disaster on Absalom. [1]

What a scene! Everyone in the room is a traitor except Hushai. He is
David's trusted man, planted there to subvert.

The story raises the question of what Reformed theology calls
the providence of God. The Swiss Reformed Church has a motto that
reads: "In the midst of human confusion, the providence of God." This
story reminds us that in the midst of all the confusion, words, and pride,
still Yahweh is there working his purpose out. "Yahweh had determined
to thwart Ahithophil's shrewd advice and so to bring disaster on Absalom." Providence means "to provide," and God does provide.   He
provides for good in the midst of confusion and everything else.   But
listen to the rest of the story.

David is warned and moves quickly across the Jordan river.
When Absalom does finally mobilize his troops and go after David, David
is ready. But David has said, "For my sake treat young Absalom gently."

In the battle that follows, Absalom gets his hair caught in a tree
in the forest of Ephrim and is pulled off his horse. He remains hanging
there from the tree limb, and Joab, one of the leaders of David's armies,
kills him. A runner is sent to give news to David. When the king is told
that a messenger is coming, he says, "If he is running all by himself, he
has good news to tell." But the watchman tells David that there is a
second runner coming far back, also by himself. Still David interprets
this as a bearer of good news. The first runner breathlessly tells him that

---

[1] *II Samuel* 17:1-14.

the loyal troops have won the battle and that the king is still safely in control. But David bruskly tells him to stand aside and make way for the second runner. This is how the Bible records it:

> Then the Cushite arrived. "Good news for my lord the king!" cried the Cushite. "Yahweh has vindicated your cause today by ridding you of all who rebelled against you." "Is all well with young Absalom?" the king asked the Cushite. "May the enemies of my lord the king," the Cushite answered, "and all who rebelled against you to your hurt, share the lot of that young man."
> The king shuddered. He went up to the room over the gate and burst into tears, and weeping said, "My son Absalom! My son! My son Absalom! Would I had died in your place! Absalom, my son, my son!" [2]

David later became even greater in the minds of the people. He became the "ideal King" to later generations. As his figure receded into the past, his faults were overlooked and his virtues came into their own. People saw in David a King wholly faithful to Yahweh, enjoying a unique place in Yahweh's favor.

Thus was born, in later years, in lesser time, in exile, and in subjection, the hope that David would one day come again, either in his own person or in a mighty son, and deliver Israel and once again make it head over the nations.

Ten centuries passed, and, when blind Bartimaus heard that Jesus was passing by, he began to cry out and say: "You, son of David, have mercy upon me." Thus, there lived beside the memory of that warrior prince, the memory of a good king before whom the needy cried

---

[2] *II Samuel* 18:31-19:2.

and had not been disappointed. Was this Jesus his son, come at long last to deliver them from their oppression?

*   *   *   *   *

The story of David is found in *I and II Samuel*.

Chapter Ten

THE PROBLEM WITH
REAL ESTATE

I've been reading a new book by Walter Brueggemann. It is a textual study of *Hope within History*. One of his illustrations is of going to his son's PTA and watching as members of the fifth-grade class performed a choric reading of United States history in which the children, one at a time, gave one-liners about American history. They said such things as: "George Washington is the father of our country;" "Thomas Jefferson wrote the Declaration of Independence;" "Abraham Lincoln freed the slaves and saved the Union." After each vignette, the entire fifth grade said in unison: "And America goes on forever."

Brueggemann reflects on the experience, thinking about what an odd notion of history and history-makers it involved. For instance, without exception, the so-called history-makers were white, male, American officeholders. And the refrain, "And America goes on forever," meant to Brueggemann that his son was "being instructed in ideological history presuming the absoluteness of an historical institution and a political idea."[1]

I too have been reflecting a bit on what I remember of my study of American history. As I recall, it consisted of memorizing the names of presidents, their parties, their states, and their religion, plus a list of the wars won and territories acquired. No one ever told me of John Dos Passos and his good literature, of Mother Jones championing the workers' cause, or of quite a number of others, including Presbyterian Norman Thomas. I got to realizing that there are a lot of people who have

---

[1] Walter Bruggemann, *Hope Within History*, John Knox Press, 1987, p. 10.

suffered to make our country what it is, but who never held office and never get onto the lists to be recited.

We must also beware of a "PTA-meeting" version of history and history-makers in the story of our own faith. The book of Kings, from which I read this morning is like that in many ways. We easily recite the first few Kings of Israel: Saul, the frightened one; David, the responsible one; Solomon, the profligate.

Solomon was followed by his son Rehoboam, in a royal succession that was expected by that time. Scripture tells us that the Israelites gathered at Shechem, by the sacred tree where Abraham had long ago built an altar to Yahweh, as the place of anointing to make Rehoboam king. But trouble arose. A man by the name of Jeroboam appeared on the scene and sparked a revolt.

Jeroboam had been in the court of Solomon, but had objected to Solomon's labor policy. He objected so strenuously and stood up so firmly for the common people, who had been ground down to support Solomon's extravagant scale of living, that he had to flee to Egypt to save his head.

So there was a real confrontation a real choice before the Israelites. A committee was elected to come forth and have a conference with the intended King to ask about *his* proposed administration. Among other things, they asked Rehoboam to reduce their taxes and stop forced labor on the King's projects. Rehoboam promised to give an answer within three days and wisely went to seek the advice of his father's counselors.

Solomon's extensive building had been completed, and the older men knew that there was a danger of rebellion. They advised Rehoboam: "Humor the people, treat them fairly and they will be your servants forever." But Rehoboam's younger friends, probably waiting the time when they could get some tax money for themselves, advised him not to let them off so easily. Rehoboam listened to them and said:

> My little finger is thicker than my father's loins!
> So then, my father made you bear a heavy
> burden. I will make it heavier still. My father

beat you with whips; I am going to beat you
with loaded scourges.[2]

At once the call went out: "To your tents, O Israel!" This meant
rebellion. Rehoboam ran back to Jerusalem and discovered that all the
tribes except Judah and the tiny tribe of Benjamin had turned against
him. He called together what warriors he could, but he soon recognized
the wisdom of his counsellors, who warned him not to attempt to sup-
press the rebellion.

In this way, the kingdom, united since Saul, divided in about 922
B.C. Rehoboam remained King over Judah and Benjamin, while Jeroboam was made King over "all Israel," which meant the other ten tribes.

When David first became king in about 1000 B.C., he pulled off
a great political coup by selecting as his capital a little-known town
named Jerusalem that none of the tribes had ever used. He consolidated
his government there on top of the mountains. Then, to further secure
it, he built a place for the Ark of the Covenant and had it brought there.
In that way, everyone had to come to Jerusalem, not only for their
governmental work, but also to worship at least once a year.

Solomon had improved on this by building a grandiose temple
and staffing it with a lot of clergy, so Jeroboam realized that if he was
going to keep the ten tribes from disaffecting, he had also to have a
temple. Thus, he not only established his capital at Shechem, but also
built a temple there, and put into it some things that really were not part
of the Israelite tradition. He also selected as priests persons who were
not of the tribe of Levi, and that was seen as breaking the clergy union.

Some of the prophets who were in the north at that time spoke
out against Jeroboam, saying "You're messing around with our religion,
and that's not right."

After Jeroboam, there follows a period of about fifty years with
a whole succession of Kings, and the PTA version of our faith's history
and history-makers lists them, like our listing of Buchanan, Millard
Fillmore, and others like them. But nothing much really happened until
a man by the name of Ahab and his wife, Jezebel, came on the scene.

---

[2] *I Kings* 12:10-11.

Jezebel was a Phoenician princess whom Ahab had come to know. Her father was a priest of the god Baal, and she was, therefore, a priestess of Baal and a princess of Phoenicia. She proved to be a complete tyrant.

She had her husband build a temple to Baal and put an image of the new goddess in the new capitol of Shechem. Scripture records that:

> Ahab did more to provoke the Lord, the God of
> Israel, to anger than all the kings of Israel who
> were before him.

The religion of Yahweh became mingled with that of Baal, and things went from bad to worse. Remember that the Israelites had come in from the desert where they had lived in tents of black goat hair and their lives had been harsh and hard. Yahweh had shared this life with them, protected them on the move, and encouraged them in battle. Now they were in the land of "milk and honey," but they soon discovered that they had to wrest a living from the soil as farmers. As they changed from wanderers in the desert to agriculturists, new methods had to be learned, and they borrowed tools, customs, habits, and religion. This was a contest between two cultures. Their native religion was almost completely concerned with the material prosperity of its adherents, and these religious concepts were challenged by a rough, courageous spokesman for God by the name of Elijah.

Elijah was a rugged outdoorsman from Galilee, and all his life he never once hesitated to speak up to King Ahab! As a matter of fact, the first thing Elijah did was to announce that Yahweh had said there would be no rain for three years in order to prove that Yahweh and not Baal was the God of nature.

The drought came, and it was a "complete drought." The King was pretty angry about it, because it was bringing down some of his economic policies, so he asked to have a meeting with Elijah. They met, and each accused the other of being responsible for the drought.

Elijah proposed a contest to see who was the mighty God, Yahweh or Baal, and Ahab agreed. The site of the demonstration was chosen by Elijah, and a dramatic setting it was, and is. Mt. Carmel is a ridge about fifteen miles long, extending into the Mediterranean and

reaching a height at the water of about 1,800 feet.   On the appointed
day, some four hundred prophets of Baal, and the King, the court, the
people, and Elijah gathered there for the big event.   Elijah lectured the
people:

> How long will you go limping with two different
> opinions.   Choose this day who is to be your
> God, Yahweh or Baal.

Having put it on the line, the contest began. Elijah and the prophets of
Baal each prepared two altars with wood upon them.   Then each cut a
bull into pieces and put it on the wood.   But no fire was to be put to the
wood; that would come from the true God.   All morning the Baal group
called upon Baal for fire and went through their dance and got no
answer.   Elijah mocked them by telling them to yell louder, Baal must
be asleep, or musing, or on a journey!   They kept up their pleading well
into the afternoon, but to no avail.

Then it was Elijah's turn.   He had the people bring forth four
jars of water and pour it on the sacrifice and the wood.   Then he had it
doused with four more jars of water, and then a third time until the
water was running off and down the hill in a small stream.   Then came
the dramatic moment.   Listen as I read it from the record:

> Elijah stepped forward.   "Yahweh, God of
> Abraham, Isaac and Israel," he said, "let them
> know today that you are God in Israel, and that
> I am your servant, that I have done all these
> things at your command. Answer me, Yahweh,
> answer me, so that this people may know that
> you, Yahweh, are God and are winning back
> their hearts."
> Then the fire of Yahweh fell and consumed
> the holocaust and wood and licked up the water
> in the trench. When all the people saw this they
> fell on their faces. "Yahweh is God," they cried,
> "Yahweh is God."   Elijah said, "Seize the pro-

phets of Baal: do not let one of them escape."
They seized them, and Elijah took them down
to the wadi Kishon, and he slaughtered them
there. [3]

But the story of Ahab, Jezebel and Elijah goes on. The struggle
between the concepts of the Phoenicians and those of Israel did not stop
with religious matters; it involved real estate as well. The Israelites,
remember, had come in from the desert where no one owned the land.
The tribes merely settled for a time in certain sections. When they came
into this land of Canaan, they brought this concept with them. They felt
that Yahweh owned the land and allowed them to use it for a time.
Each tribe was allocated a section which was divided in turn among the
clans.   Each clan divided the territory among the families, and the
families made assignments to individual members. As people died, their
sons took their places, and in this way, each one was assured some land
to use. He could not sell it, for he did not own it; he could not lose it for
debt, he could not even give it away, for he did not own it.

But Jezebel came from a people with a different set of concepts.
Her people made their living buying and selling. They were a seagoing
people, and, because they moved about so much, they built up little love
for particular spots. So Jezebel could not appreciate the Israelite attitude
toward real estate.

Near Ahab's palace there was a vineyard of a man named
Naboth. Ahab offered to buy the vineyard or to give Naboth a better one
in exchange for it. But Naboth, a conservative Israelite, clung to the
older idea that property was owned by Yahweh and merely assigned for
his use, and he said he had no right to sell it. Ahab was angry about this.
but he recognized Naboth's right.

However, Jezebel would not stand for what she saw as Jewish
foolishness, so she forged the King's name to orders that Naboth be
charged with cursing God and the King, and that he be stoned to death
for the crime. And he was.

---

[3] *I Kings* 18:36-40.

When Ahab heard of Naboth's death, he went to take possession of the vineyard. There he was met by (you guessed it) Elijah! Elijah told Ahab that: "In the place where dogs licked up the blood of Naboth shall dogs lick your own blood." And that came true!

The whole story is here to teach us that Yahweh is interested in justice. Ethics had largely been dropped from the religion of Israel, and this theme was constantly re-emphasized by Elijah, but there is something more embedded in this saga. The evil course of Ahab seemed to reach its depth in his killing of Naboth in order to get possession of a vineyard, and it teaches us something about the selling of one's soul. His petty greed, his pliability in Jezebel's unscrupulous hands, his permission of the trumped-up charge against Naboth, and his complicity in the execution of the innocent man, all add up to a chapter of blackness. What a complete denial of ethics! No wonder that when he saw Elijah approaching he cried, "Have you found me, O my enemy?"

To a guilty conscience the prophet of God always looks like an enemy, and Elijah replied: "I have found you because you have sold yourself to what it evil." He had sold his soul for the price of his neighbor's vineyard. That is the problem with real estate (or anything else, for that matter); when possessions possess us, they can blind us to the consequences of our actions. It is very easy to start on that progression, giving up integrity bit by bit, losing possession of our soul by mortgaging it bit by bit. Someone "gets something on us," and that gives them a hold over us, like a mortgage on our person. In the presence of some people, we cannot call our soul our own because we have done things which keep us from being our true selves. We become someone else and are no longer true to our beliefs, thoughts, and feelings; we live a lie to get false acceptance, and we die. The process of selling one's soul is subtle. We can lose it just by being quiet, when we discover that silence is golden because it pays profits in popularity.

I once accused a U.S. diplomat of being silent in six languages, while he rationalized his cowardice by calling it diplomacy, discretion, and tact. In fact he lost his soul and the leadership possibility that went with it. How about others of us who are corporate officers? How are we to be loyal to employees, stockholders, *and* the general public? As citizens of the United States, how are we to be loyal to a country that protects us, yet not sell out to policies that are wrong.

Elijah comes through here to remind us that the principle is to have a loyalty which goes beyond all other loyalties: to Yahweh, to our God, to our God of the desert. As Jesus said: "Put first the Kingdom of God." The testimony of our mothers and fathers in the faith is that it works. Elijah put it bluntly in our story for this day:

> How long will you hobble first on one leg and then on the other. Choose you this day. If Yahweh is God, follow him. If Baal, follow him!

*   *   *   *   *

The story of Elijah is told in *I Kings* 17, through *II Kings* 2:13.

Chapter Eleven

HOT ROD IN THE VALLEY

I told Kay that if we didn't go to Carolyn Kennedy's wedding one week, we couldn't go to Fergie and Andy's the next; it just wouldn't be right. But millions did. Millions sat glued to the TV to watch Fergie and Andy do their thing at Westminster Abby.

As a preliminary there were lots of shows about royal weddings, and one reminded me of how important royal weddings really are. It pointed out how Queen Victoria and her German consort Albert populated the whole of Europe with cousins, and that the First World War was indeed a family feud. Gaining territory, power, and control has been the motivation behind most royal weddings, not just in Europe, but in the Bible as well, and the effects of those biblical marriages were no better than in the recent past, as we shall see in this "bible story that you never heard before."

For this story we turn to the two books in the Old Testament, I and II Kings. These books and I & II Samuel, were originally one; they were separated for convenience in reading the long scrolls on which they were written. Their original Hebrew title was *Concerning the Kingdoms*. Our key date for this story is 1000 B.C., when David was King in Israel. He was followed by his son Solomon and by Bathsheba. After that a civil war divided the nation into two parts, the Northern Kingdom, called Israel, and the Southern Kingdom, called Judah. Our story is centered in the Northern Kingdom of Israel and comes from the book of II Kings, probably the most political of all the books of the Bible. It was a time of crisis in the nation, and we see politics in action, not just in principle.

The theologian Karl Barth said that this book displays most concretely the free determination of man in the free decision of God. We live in the tension between our actions and God's actions. Most believe in God's ultimate destiny for us, but also believe that God does not make puppets of us, but gives us free play. On the other hand, as Treve in *Fiddler on the Roof* would say, we are not free; we are under the burden and control of our body and our passion, the conditioning of our society and culture. We are controlled by our situation and our psychology; we really are not free. These are the facts which II Kings brings before us, particularly in the incident of our story today. In it, we will see human beings deciding on a great number of actions freely and alone. Many of them will fall, they are nonsensical and they missfire to be lost in the sand. But some succeed, and when they do, they enter into God's design and ultimately bring about the destiny that Yahweh has in mind for us all.

But do not be deceived. In this relationship between God's decisions and our decisions, we must not be content with too simple a scheme. The relationship between them can be complex and torturous, and is easily misinterpreted and misunderstood.

The whole life of the Israelites was one of trying to understand their relationship to this mysterious Yahweh who had called to Abraham and Sarah so long ago, who had, in so many ways and places, led them, guided them, and guarded them. The prophets, good teachers, kept flinging their arms back and telling the people to remember. Remember, they said, how Abraham and Sarah, your mother and father in the faith, left Ur and walked that thousand miles to the promised land they had never seen. Remember Isaac and Rebecca, Jacob and Rachael, and their hardships with settling in the new land of Canaan. Remember the famine, the going to Egypt. Remember the words of Moses to Pharaoh, "let my people go." Remember the passage with Miriam through the Red sea; remember the giving of the law, Joshua, and the Judges. Remember, remember, remember.

Their teaching was a continual lesson in the development of a political system. Under Moses, the people had a military dictator, who whipped them into an effective army to do what was necessary in those days. This continued under Joshua, but as they settled down, Judges arose, strong charismatic war lords who could raise an army quickly to put down the pockets of resistance, and keep a link between the tribes as they continued to settle.

Soon the people also began to look and listen to the nations around them with whom they had trade and commerce, and they began to ask, "Why don't we have a king like other people have kings?" They badgered the prophet Samuel to get them one. But Samuel was not sold on the idea and said that God did not want them to have a king, that Yahweh was their king and no one in any way should erode that loyalty and understanding.

But the people moaned and complained and pushed and shoved until finally Samuel said "all right, already," and anointed Saul as the first King of Israel.

Saul was a fearful, cautious, superstitious, tight man, utterly controlled by what he considered to be the powers, principalities, demons, and devils of the world. He was followed by David, who understood the interaction of living in God's world creatively and yet giving awe to God in his mysterious power.

David was a person of the people. He lived an earthy life and yet also had a strong understanding of Yahweh. His devotion and loyalty were unquestionable even in the midst of his sin.

But his son, Solomon, was quite different. Where Saul, the first king, had been powerless in the sense that he was controlled by the fate of demons and threatened by ghosts and goblins, Solomon took it to the other extreme; he cared nothing for God at all. He was a politician without a conscience. He misunderstood David's devotion to his God and sensitivity to the needs of the people. So after Solomons' death the kingdom was divided into two, and two kings succeeded Solomon, Reahaboam in the south and Jeraboam in the North. It was about halfway between the dividing of the Kingdom in 930 and the fall of the Northern Kingdom in 730 B.C. that our story takes place.

The setting of the story is magnificent, and you can still go to the city of Nazareth and sit on the south slope of the mountain on which the city is built; there spread out before you is the beautiful plain of Jezreal. When I sat there, I thought of all the battles that had been fought within my sight, for this is one of the crossroads of the ancient world.

In the distance is the little town of Jezreal. It was a royal city in the time of Ahab, King of the North, and Ahab and his wife Jezebel came there often. Near the town of Jezreal was a vineyard owned by a man called Naboth. King Ahab offered to buy the vineyard, but Naboth, in conservative Israelite style, believed the property had been assigned to him by his father and that morally he had no right to sell it. The King was vexed and sullen about this, but he recognized Naboth's right. Listen to the exchange:

> Naboth of Jezreel had a vineyard close by the palace of Ahab, King of Samaria, and Ahab said to Naboth, "Give me your vineyard to be my vegetable garden, since it adjoins my house; I will give you a better vineyard for it or, if you prefer, I will give you its worth in money." But Naboth answered Ahab, "Yahweh forbid that I should give you the inheritance of my ancestors!"
>
> Ahab went home gloomy and out of temper at the words of Naboth of Jezreel, "I will not give you the inheritance of my fathers." He lay down on his bed and turned his face away and refused to eat. His wife Jezebel came to him. "Why are you so dispirited" she said "That you will not eat?" He said, "I have been speaking to Naboth of Jezreel; I said: Give me your vineyard either for money or, if you prefer, for another vineyard in exchange. But he said, 'I will not give you may vineyard'." Then his wife Jezebel said, "You make a fine King of Israel, and no mistake! Get up and eat; cheer up, and you will feel better; I will get you the vineyard of Naboth of Jezreel myself." [1]

Jezebel would not stand for any of what she considered Israelite foolishness. She was, I forgot to tell you, a foreign woman, a royal marriage made to keep peace with the Phoenicians. She forged the King's name to orders that Naboth be charged with cursing God and the King and that he be stoned to death for the crime. So it was done.

---

[1] *I Kings* 21:1-7.

When Ahab heard of Naboth's death he went to take possession of the vineyard. There he was met by the prophet Elijah who warned him, "In the place where dogs lick up the blood of Naboth shall dogs lick your own blood."

I tell you this vignette to illustrate that that time in Israel was a time of lying, cheating, deceiving, murder, theft, and intrigue, whether King, Queen or common peasant; it was a time of worship of the pagan god Baal; but it was a time of no ethics.

Well toward the end of his life the prophet Elijah was told by Yahweh to go find a new king and anoint him. But Elijah died and it fell to his disciple, Elisha, to fulfill the assignment. By this time Jehoram, the son of Ahab was King, and he had been trying to gain a city from the Syrians. The fighting was long, and the king was tired. He left his general, Jehu, in command and returned to Jezreal. Elisha came to Jehu in his camp and poured a flask of holy oil on him, anointing him King of Israel. At this his officers spread their cloaks under him, sounded the trumpets and shouted, "Jehu is king!"

As soon as Jehu discovered that the other generals, officers and soldiers were willing to support him as king, he mounted his chariot and rode through the valley to Jezreal to carry out the revolution. And what a ride it was! He was known as a fast charioteer and you can imagine the dust cloud that followed this hot rod! Scripture tells us that the watchman, high up on a lookout on the walls of Jezreal, spotted Jehu coming (who could miss that one!) and ran to tell the King.

The King sent out a horseman to meet him and ask whether all was well. When the horseman asked the King's question, Jehu replied: "What has it to do with you whether all is well? Fall in behind me."

The watchman reported that the messenger had reached them but was not coming back, so the King sent a second horseman. He too asked the King's question, and again Jehu replied: "What has it to do with you whether all is well? Fall in behind me."

Once again the watchman reported that the horseman had reached them but was not coming back, and he went on to say that the manner of driving was like that of Jehu, who drove like a madman.

At that the king called for his chariot, and with a bodyguard, set out to meet Jehu. They met in the field of Nabaoth, and there Jehu declared his rebellion.

The king asked, "Is all well, Jehu?" And Jehu replied: "What a question, when all the while the prostitution and countless sorceries of your mother Jezebel go on!" He declared that there would be no peace as long as the way of life exemplified by Jezebel was allowed to mold the way of government. At this Jehoram wheeled and began to flee, calling out "treason." But Jehu drew his bow and struck Jehoram between the shoulder blades. The arrow went through the King's heart, and he sank in his chariot. Jehu said:

> Pick him up, and throw him into the field of Nabaoth. Remember how, when you and I both rode behind Ahab his father, Yahweh pronounced this sentence against him, so pick him up and throw him into the field as Yahweh declared should happen.[2]

Again the chariots began to move swiftly through the valley to Jezreal. By this time, Jezebel must have known what had taken place. She had outlived three kings, her husband and two sons, and she thought she knew how to handle men. Jezebel stepped out upon the balcony of her palace to meet the oncoming horde. In preparation she had bathed and perfumed her body, applied cosmetics, and made a careful coiffure of her hair.

As Jehu stood staring up at the infamous queen, his clothes stained with the blood of her son, she taunted him. Jehu replied with a smile which seemed to ask if regicide was the only sort of murder to which royalty objected. Jehu called up to her, "Who is on my side? Who?" When others looked out, he shouted: "Throw her out!" and they threw her down. She hit the pavement and was trampled by the horses.

Jehu went in to eat and drink, but then recalled that Jezebel was the daughter of a king and deserved a decent burial. "See to this ac-

---

[2] *II Kings* 9:25-26.

cursed woman, and give her decent burial," he ordered. But when they went to bury her, they found little, for the dogs had destroyed most of her body (even as it had been foretold by the prophet Elijah many years before).

Jehu's next move was to have all the sons of Ahab decapitated, thus removing all claimants to the throne. Then, in an interesting move, Jehu called together all the people of the city and said,

> Men of Israel, people, simple people, you are
> innocent. What has happened is not your doing
> you have had no hand in it, I myself am guilty.
> I conspired against my master and slew him.[3]

We must, in the midst of this gory tale, give Jehu his due. He was just as strict with himself as with others. His final act was to destroy the leaders of the Baal worship. He gathered them all together feigning his devotion to Baal. They were all gathered in a Baal temple, and he sent in his soldiers and destroyed them all and converted the pagan temple into a public privy.

It's quite a story, thoughnot a pretty one, and perhaps not one we want to think about being in the bible. But that is what, to me, gives the Bible such authenticity. It does not cover up, and no later, more sensitive and enlightened soul decided to leave out this or that particular story, or alter it, or smooth it to make it more palatable. And there are things we can learn from it.

One thing is what can happen when someone, even from genuine religious motivation, is convinced that they alone know the will of God. Far too often and in much less dramatic ways than Jehu, a person may become convinced that they alone know how to fulfill what they conceive as God's design for the world, or a group of persons, or an individual. Then they begin to try to shape history in the name of God, but also in the place of God.

I am sure that Jehu was a truly religious man. I am certain that he and his generals were sick of the low standards of the King and his

---

[3] *II Kings* 10:8-9.

family, of the idolatry of Ahab, of the worship of bloodthirsty gods who demanded and were given human sacrifices, of the magical forces unleashed by Jezebel, and of the violence of Ahab in his massacre of the believers in Yahweh. All this set in motion a logical sequence of events whose flame finally blew back and consumed Ahab himself.

But Jehu gave into the temptation to make it happen. He gave in to the temptation of too many politicians of his time and since, to use prophecy in the interest of politics while pretending to use politics in the service of prophecy. Jehu thinks Yahweh speaks and then abdicates, and that he, Jehu, has full decision and control after that. But the living God, the Yahweh of the whole Bible, does not announce and then leave the means to others. It is not just the end that Yahweh cares about, it is the means as well.

Jehu decided to be king and make the people faithful to God. He used political means to force the people into this faithfulness, to force people to a certain perception through laws and the power of government. And that, to put it mildly, is what leads to misunderstanding, or to a Jonestown in Guyana.

But one thing more from this story. Force is a poor weapon with which to combat ideas. Jehu's attempt to eradicate Baal worship released the forces of a fanatic revolution. Famine and death stalked the land, every foreign element in it was attacked, courts were arbitrarily set up, and enemies both real and fancied were put to the sword. Bloodthirsty fanatics, narrow in their outlook and primitive in their methods, are seldom successful in running a government. Lacking political experience, the bigoted rulers of Israel sought isolation, refusing to enter into agreements with their neighbors east or west.

Jehu isolated himself from the Southern Kingdom, and his slaughter of the worshipers of the Phoenician Baal cut off any support from Phonecia. So the Northern Kingdom was more vulnerable to attack from Syria, and Hazael, the Syrian King, was quick to take advantage of the situation. He swept down from the heights and through this same valley of Jezreal. Jehu sensed his hopeless plight and, anxious to save his throne at any cost, paid tribute to the Syrian monarch Shalmaneser III. This political event is ignored in the biblical account but it is known to us; it is part of the depiction and inscription of the famous Black Obelisk of Shalmaneser III, which shows Jehu kneeling before Shalmaneser, and Shalmaneser receiving tribute from the King of Israel.

*   *   *   *   *

The story of Jehu is told in *II Kings* 9-10.

Chapter Twelve

BLOOD, SWEAT, AND TEARS

Sometimes, though not always, individuals and nations are given a second chance. The Jews have been especially fortunate in this regard. By this time you know well how it all began with Abraham and Sarah in about 1725 B.C., when they were told to take a thousand-mile walk to the country called Canaan. Then came a whole series of "second chances." Forced to flee to Egypt because of famine, they fell under bondage to the pharaoh, but Moses and Miriam led them out to freedom again. They crossed the Marsh Sea, made a covenant with Yahweh at Sinai, and wandered in the wilderness. Then Joshua led them to the land of Canaan again, they conquered it, and settled down under the Judges.

David became King in about 1000 B.C. and his son Solomon built a temple to house the Ark of the Covenant. They grew strong as a nation, but after Solomon the kingdom was divided. The Northern Kingdom was carried into captivity by the Assyrians, and sometime later the Southern Kingdom was carried into captivity by the Babylonians who had taken over the "world" from the Assyrians.

From a human point of view it would seem that at this point the history of the chosen people had ended. The northern tribes who were carried into captivity did indeed abandon their religion and were absorbed into the neighboring population. Their role in history was virtually completed. But the Southern kingdom, called Judah, was quite different.

The Jews in Judah were inspired by a series of outstanding prophets; Isaiah, Jeremiah, Ezekiel. They retained their religion and their national identity, even in captivity by Babylon.

Finally, as prophets had proclaimed, came their second chance, though not all at once. The new nation was not rebuilt in a day, or a year, or even a generation. We sometimes forget that there are long lapses between the events recorded in the history of our mothers and fathers in the faith.

Jerusalem was completely destroyed by the Babylonians under Nebuchadnezzar in the year 587 B.C. For fifty years it lay waste, but then a great change occurred on the global scene of history. Up until this time, the history of the area from eastern Mediterranean to the country we now call India had been controlled by people we call Semites. But now, the Medes swept down out of the high plateaus of the land we now call Iran, attacked Nineveh, gained possession of the Assyrian lands, and conquered the Babylonians.

In 538 B.C. a Persian king came to power, and brought a new concept of civilization to peoples as far away as the Mediterranean and Egypt. Remember that up until this time when a nation was conquered, it was customary to remove from the territory of the conquered nation, the leaders, artisans, craftspersons, decision makers, and anyone who might be able to organize and lead an army. They were taken into exile, back to the homeland of the conqueror. The peasants were left on the land to plant and harvest crops and send taxes or tribute to the conqueror.

Gathered by the River of Babylon therefore, were Israel's finest people. They learned the techniques of survival in a foreign land. They even discovered, through the help of a prophet called Second Isaiah, that Yahweh did not have to be worshipped only in Jerusalem, but could be worshipped even in this foreign land.

Then came a most startling change. In the very first year of the reign of the Persian Cyrus, a royal decree was issued that granted permission for all of Yahweh's people who wished to do so to return to their land and rebuild Jerusalem. A second decree announced that the Jews who preferred to remain, would help their people who wished to return with money, goods, and beasts.

The news of these proclamations must have run through the empire like wildfire. It stirred the Jews to a frenzy of activity. They felt that their dreams had become realities, their prophecies fulfillments.

What many fail to realize is that most of the Jews preferred to remain in Babylon where they had established themselves. Only a minority took advantage of Cyrus' generous offer; the Bible tells us that only about 42,000 persons made the trip under the leadership of a grandson of one of the last kings of Judah, a man named Zerubbabel.

These returning exiles did not find their former land unoccupied. On the contrary, they had to settle down in the midst of a foreign population, and the people living on the land took a dim view of the Jews returning. Philistines had pressed into Judah from the west, Amonites and Moabites came from the east, and Edomites from the South. Whole villages which had been Jewish were now gentile, as was Jerusalem itself.

The walls of Jerusalem had been torn down, the houses destroyed, and the temple burned. The massive foundations of the temple laid by Solomon probably suffered little, but they were all that remained. The first public act of the returned community was to erect an altar and the make a burnt offering on the site of the old temple. Then they began to rebuild the temple.

They had to quarry new stone and secure wood from Lebanon. It was costly and difficult. Great trees had to be felled and dragged over the crest of the Lebanon mountains, slid down the side, rafted to Joppa and dragged on up to Jerusalem. It was a big undertaking for people so poor. But masons and carpenters were put to work with great enthusiasm and so it proceeded.

When the foundation was completed there was an elaborate celebration. The singing was done by two great choirs. Often they sang antiphonally, one singing, "O give thanks to the Lord for he is good," the other responding, "for His mercy endureth forever." The people gave themselves in wholehearted celebration and shouted with such abandon that the noise was heard afar. Heard, for instance, by the Samaritans and others not happy that they had returned.

But the little colony did not prosper. There was little or no increase in population, and most found it difficult to make a living. They began to rebuild the walls without which no city could survive in those days. But the Samaritans, always at odds with the Jews, kept raiding them, and stealing their goods and supplies. The surrounding nations inflicted many injuries on the Jews; they overran the country and plundered it by day and did much mischief by night. Many persons had were carried off as captives from the country and from Jerusalem itself, and every day the roads were full of corpses. The colony was in a very desperate plight, and we come now to the story of Nehemiah.

Nehemiah was a wealthy and influential Jew in Babylon. He was one of the cup-bearers of the king. We don't know exactly what sort of an office this was, but it is clear that it was a post of great importance. Nehemiah had received news that the rebuilding of Jerusalem was not going well, and he was greatly disturbed. He was so distressed that it even showed in his face when he was in the presence of the King; the King, expecting only smiling faces about him, asked him what the trouble was.

Nehemiah told him about the unhappy report from Jerusalem. The King obviously cared a great deal for Nehemiah, for he not only gave Nehemiah permission to go back to Jerusalem and get things straightened out there, he also gave him practically a blank check on the King's building supplies not far from Jerusalem.

Nehemiah eagerly went back to Jerusalem, and was shocked to discover that the situation was, if anything, worse than reported. He found that the people who had remained on land while others were in exile were satisfied with things as they were and wanted nothing changed. They were running things from neighboring Samaria, and they did not want Jerusalem rebuilt and set up as a principal city in competition. So Nehemiah prepared for trouble from the very start. He rounded up all the people who were really interested and set each one to work where the wall was closest to his own home. In that way each one could see the value of what he was doing.

When those from Samaria saw that the work was proceeding well, they threatened serious trouble. So Nehemiah had every person armed as he worked; some of them worked with a tool in one hand and a weapon in the other. Later, when things grew still tighter, half the men stood guard while the rest worked. Nehemiah kept a trumpeter always by his side to sound the signal in case of trouble. They worked, "From the beginning of the dawn until the stars appeared." So through blood, and sweat, and tears, the wall was rebuilt and Jerusalem once more became a city.

What a leader Nehemiah must have been to carry with him a whole discouraged community and undertake what for their slender resources must have been a huge task.

Finally, all that remained was to dedicate the walls. The story of how this was done is told in the twelfth chapter of the book that carries Nehemiah's name. Nehemiah divided the princes of Judah into two groups and told them to lead the way in opposite directions around the top of the new wall. Each group was followed by a great company of people in was a joyful procession, the people shouting thanksgiving, and the event enlivened by the music of cymbals and trumpets. The two groups met at last in the temple enclosure and stood there, the music bursting forth in triumphant gratitude while great sacrifices were offered to Yahweh.

And so Jerusalem was given a second chance to be established in glory; once again it was the center of the worshipping community. Credit must be given to Nehemiah as a true and able leader. He was a stern disciplinarian and yet also exceedingly sensitive. One of the beautiful things about him was his care for the poor. In reading the book you get the impression that time after time he stood with the common people against the powerful moneyed groups of the community.

One last thing about Nehemiah. He was not a priest or a prophet, but a business man. He was sure that for every problem there was a solution just as simple as getting men to work by having each one build the wall near his own house. Nehemiah did his work and returned to Babylon, but he left his stamp upon the future; he set the scene for Zechariah to preach:

> Yahweh Sabaoth says this. I am coming back to Zion and shall dwell in the middle of Jerusalem. Jerusalem will be called Faithful City and the mountain of Yahweh Sabaoth, the Holy Mountain.
>
> Yahweh Sabaoth says this. Old men and old women will again sit down in the squares of Jerusalem; every one of them staff in hand

because of their great age. And the squares of the city will be full of boys and girls playing.

Yahweh Sabaoth says this. Now I am going to save my people from the countries of the East and from the countries of the West. I will bring them back to live inside Jerusalem. They shall be my people and I will be their God in faithfulness and integrity.[1]

Nehemiah set the scene for Micah to prophecy:

In the days to come the mountain of the Temple of Yahweh will be put on top of the mountains and be lifted higher than the hills. The peoples will stream to it, nations without number will come to it; and they will say, "Come, let us go up to the mountain of Yahweh, to the Temple of the God of Jacob so that he may teach us his ways and we may walk in his paths; . . . He will wield authority over many peoples and arbitrate for mighty nations: they will hammer their swords into ploughshares, their spears into sickles. Nation will not lift sword against nation, there will be no more training for war. Each one will sit under his vine and his fig tree, with no one to trouble him.[2]

Four centuries later, Jesus drew near these walls of Jerusalem. He sent for a colt and quoted Zechariah, "Behold your king is coming to you, humble and mounted on an ass and on a colt, the foal of an ass."

---

[1] *Zechariah* 8:3-8.

[2] *Micah* 4:1-4.

He went into that city through those walls on that first Palm Sunday and enacted a parable of the love of God.

*   *   *   *   *

The story of Nehemiah is found in the book by that name in the Bible.

Chapter Thirteen

PATRIOT WITHOUT A PETTICOAT

Well once more the Fourth of July has come and gone, with all the usual sun, suds and fireworks, but with little, if any, patriotic oratory. No one mentioned Molly Hays, for instance. You never heard of her? How about by her nickname, Molly Pitcher?

During the American Revolution, Molly Hays took a pitcher of cool water up and down the firing lines to assist the men in battle, and when her husband fell mortally wounded, she ripped a piece from her petticoat and offered it to be used for cannon wadding. She became one in a long line of gallant women who have been actively involved in acts of patriotism.

I could also mention that great Frenchwoman, Charlotte Corday, whose act of patriotism was to force her way into the home of Jean-Paul Marat, the most blood-thirsty of the French terrorists, and stab him to death in his bathtub. Or I could mention Jael, who is enshrined in the song of Deborah, a bedouin woman who used her guile against Sisera; she brought out a pitcher of milk, which was a sign of hospitality, to Sisera, the leader of a force against her people. When he bent down to drink it, she shoved a tent peg through his head.

But, instead of these or other possible candidates, I want to turn to the story of Judith, as told in the book of Judith in the Apocrypha.

The story was written in the time of the Maccabean Revolt, but it is set years before at the time of an invasion by the Assyrians. We are told that the whole Assyrian army, infantry, cavalry, and chariots had kept the small Israeli town of Bethulia blockaded for thirty-four days before this amazing woman named Judith came on the scene. Here is the story as told in the Bible:

> News of what was happening reached Judith.
> . . . Her husband Manassas, who belonged to

her own tribe and clan, had died at the time of
barley harvest. While he was out in the fields
supervising the binding of the sheaves, he got
sunstroke, took to his bed, and died in Bethulia
his native town; and they buried him beside his
ancestors in the field between Dothan and
Balamon. For three years and four months
Judith had lived at home as a widow; she had a
shelter erected on the roof of her house; she
put on sackcloth and always wore mourning.
After she became a widow she fasted every day
except sabbath eve, the sabbath itself, the eve of
the new moon, the new moon, and the Israelite
feasts and days of public rejoicing. She was a
very beautiful and attractive woman. Her
husband Manassas had left her gold and silver,
male and female slaves, livestock and land, and
she lived on her estate. No one spoke ill of
her, for she was a very devout woman. [1]

As the story begins, Nebuchadnezzar was the ruler of the world,
as he modestly called himself, and he ruled from the city of Nineveh.
But some of the nations he ruled didn't take him very seriously and failed
to send proper money and men for his armies. So he decided to march
west and destroy all the western nations that had flaunted his request for
money and men.

He charged one of his five-star generals, Holofernes, to do the
job. Holofernes was to take 120,000 foot soldiers and 12,000 calvary and
move west and ravage the lands and destroy all the local gods so that all
who were left would worship only Nebuchadnezzar.

Holofernes did well. The cities of Tyre, Sidon, Jamnia, and
Ascalon gave in, and the victorious army demolished all the shrines,
demanding that the subjected people should henceforth worship Nebuchadnezzar alone as god.

---

[1] *Judith* 8:1-8.

But then he hit a road block. The people of Israel in Judah heard of the atrocities of Holofernes, and, fearful that he would despoil their temple in Jerusalem, they determined to block his advance. They mobilized forces and provisions at strategic passes in the hills to the north of Jerusalem.

When Holofernes found out that there were people who were actually going to oppose him, he was enraged. He gathered the local intelligence network and asked some questions. It was poor Achior, a leader of the Ammonites, who brought him the message. He recited the history of the Israelites from Abraham and Sarah on, telling him of the special relationship they had to their God, Yahweh. He told how they seemed invincible, so long as they followed the commandments of Yahweh and did not sin. I suppose that this might have been the first time in history that the bearer of bad news really got himself in trouble from just speaking the bad news. Holofernes was so angry at what he heard, that he ordered Achior bound and staked at the foot of the hill before the village that stood in his way. The people of Bethulia found Achior, took him inside, and brought him before the elders. Achior told his story and was treated kindly by Uzziah, the ruler of the city. Then Holofernes moved his whole army into the valley by Bethulia, filling the inhabitants with terror. He decided not to attack but to cut off the water supply and wait until thirst and famine would force the Jews to surrender.

Thirty-four days went by. The source of water dried up, the cisterns went dry, and the people fainted from thirst and were falling in the streets. They accused the elders of the town of having caused their plight and demanded that they surrender the city. The elders appealed to them to be patient saying,

> Courage, let us hold out for five days more in
> which our God will turn his mercy toward us.
> Yahweh will not forsake us. If no help comes
> in five days we will surrender.

When Judith heard of this, being rich as well as beautiful, she summoned the elders to her home and indignantly chewed them out for attempting to force Yahweh's hand. "Listen to me," she said:

You had no right to speak as you did to the people today, and to bind yourselves by oath before God to surrender the town to our enemies if the Lord sends no relief within so many days. Who are you to test God at a time like this, and openly set yourselves above him? You are putting the Lord Almighty to the proof. You will never understand! You cannot plumb the depths of the human heart or understand the way a man's mind works; how then can you fathom man's Maker? How can you know God's mind, and grasp his thought? No, my friends, do not rouse the anger of the Lord our God. for even if he does not choose to help us within the five days, he is free to come to our rescue at any time he pleases, or equally to let us be destroyed by our enemies. It is not for you to impose conditions on the Lord our God; God will not yield to threats or be bargained with like mere man. So we must wait for him to deliver us, and in the mean time appeal to him for help. If he does fit he will hear us.[2]

You see she was a Presbyterian. She practically invented the saying, "Pray as if everything depended on God and work as if everything depended on you." She not only had the gift to give a good convincing speech, but her prayer afterward was superb, and after the prayer, she worked.

After she prayed, she took off her widow's mourning clothes, washed, anointed herself with rich perfume, did her hair up real nice, and put on her brightest clothes. She put on sandals, anklets, bracelets, and rings. She dolled up as if to catch the eye of any man who might see her.

Then she packed a goody-bag with a skin of wine, a flask of oil, barley cakes and fruits and went to the gate of the village. When the

---

[2] *Judith* 8:11-17.

guards saw her they were completely taken by her beauty. She and her maid went out of the city and down into the valley toward the camp of the enemy. There they were stopped by an Assyrian patrol.

She told them that she was getting out of the city while the getting was good and that she would be willing to tell their general how he could conquer the city. Beside being stunned by her beauty, the guards were taken in and convinced by her speech. They took her to the tent of Holofernes where she let forth with this blarney,

> We have heard how wise and clever you are.
> You are known throughout the world as the
> man of ability unrivaled in the whole empire, of
> powerful intelligence and amazing skill in the
> art of war.

He told her she had noting to worry about, only those who had refused to serve Nebuchadnezzar, like her people in the city, had any reason to fear.

Judith assured him that Achior had spoken the truth and that the Jews would come to no harm unless they sinned against God. But she said,

> You don't need to be downcast, for the sin has
> already overtaken them. They intended to take
> and eat consecrated food to ease their hunger.
> Once they do that, they will be destroyed.

Pleased by Judith's words, to say nothing of her great beauty, Holofernes asked her to stay as his guest. She accepted, but she said that she was really a very religious person and therefore had to go out of the camp each night to worship by the spring in the valley and to eat her kosher food that she kept in her goody-bag. For three days she lived in the camp, though each night she left the camp with her maid to bathe in the spring.

By the fourth day, Holofernes was out of his mind with desire for Judith, and he invited her to a banquet in his tent. Her beauty, her finery, and her wit made her the center of attraction. Finally all the officers left, and Holofernes was alone with Judith. All her plans had been laid for this moment, and here is the lesson in ethics. Is she an absolutist or a situationalist? She is ready to do adultery, but adultery for a greater loyalty, the nation, so that other lives may be saved.

Well, Holofernes was pretty sloshed by this time and fell asleep. With a prayer for strength, Judith came close to his bed, seized his sword, took hold of his hair, and struck his neck twice with all her might. She severed his head from his body. Then she gave the head to her maid to put in the goody-bag, and both women left the tent, and the camp, carrying the goodie-bag, without arousing suspicion since they had done that same routine every other night.

When Judith drew near Bethulia, she called out to the watchman, "Open the gate for the Lord our God is with us still." She went in and showed the people the bloody trophy, and there was unbounded joy in the city. She frankly acknowledge,

> My face seduced him, only to his own undoing.
> He committed no sin with me, to shame me, or
> disgrace me.

The people of Bethulia marched out at dawn and attacked. At first the Assyrians were surprised and waited impatiently for an order from the general, but they became paralyzed with fear when it was reported that the mighty Holofernes had been slain, and by a woman. The soldiers dispersed in mad terror, and the Jews pursued them and slaughtered them.

The high priest came from Jerusalem when he heard of this great feat by Judith, and blessed her. In gratitude they gave Holofernes' tent and all its contents to Judith as a gift of thanks. And Judith and all the women went dancing in the streets.

They wrote a psalm about Judith, for she was famous throughout the whole land. And the last verse of the story reads:

> No one dared to threaten the Israelites again in
> Judith's lifetime, or for a long time after her
> death.

It is a neat story, well told, a story of patriotism and ethics, written at a time of national crisis to revitalize the flagging courage and revive the faltering devotion of the people. So, on this Independence Day weekend, a note of patriotism from the distant past, and a salute to a woman, who put a marauding general in his place.

*   *   *   *   *

The story of Judith is found in the book by that name in the Apocrypha section of the Bible.

Chapter Fourteen

THE PROBLEM WITH LOVE

In Marc Connelly's play *Green Pastures*, there is a scene in which two office cleaners are looking down at the earth and watching "de Lawd" throw down thunderbolts on the population which, "has made de debbil king and dey wukkin' in three shifts fo' him." There follows this dialogue between God and Gabriel:

> *God*: Look at 'em dere. Squirmin' an' fightin' an' bearin' false witness. Listen to dat liar, dere. He don' intend to marry dat little gal. He don' even love her.

> *Gabriel*: How would it be if you was to doom 'em all ag'n, like dat time you sent down de flood? I bet dat would make dem mind.

> *God*: You see how much good de flood did. Dere dey is, jest as bad as ever.

> *Gabriel*: How about cleanin' up de whole mess of 'em and sta'tin' all over ag'in wid some new kind of animal?

> *God*: An' admit I'm licked? No, suh. No, suh. Man is a kind of pet of mine and it ain't right fo' me to give up tryin' to do somethin' wid him. Doggone, mankin' mus' be all right at the core

or else why did I ever bother wid him in de first place?[1]

So Marc Connelly testifies to God as a God of love who will not give up. That's the problem with real love; it will not admit defeat, it will not give up.

"All the world loves a lover," and most of the world loves a story about a lover. This story falls into that category, for Hosea was a lover if ever there was one. His love was so strong that even the most vile behavior could not dull it. He suffered severely but in each pang of suffering he came to know the infinite heart of God more dearly. Hosea's wife, Gomar bat-Diblaim, broke his heart, but she made it possible for Hosea to give to us, and to all the world, a picture of the heart of the God of love.   Here is the setting.

Jeroboam II was on the throne as King in Israel. It was an era of peace, plenty, prosperity, and luxury. Both in Samaria and Jerusalem, the people indulged in the kind of living that weakened and debauched them. They drifted thoughtlessly into ease, extravagance, and oppression.

The prophet Amos came on the scene to preach to them, but even his burning message had little effect upon the people; they could not see any evidence of the consequences that this prophet predicted. Things were too peaceful for them to observe the reality of their situation.

But, Jeroboam was soon succeeded by his son, Zechariah, and Zechariah was murdered, after only six months, by Shallum. Shallum lasted only eight days until he was murdered by Menahem. So Menahem became King and reigned by political intrigue and murder.

The political instability of the period was also reflected in social instability. Property had little value, for no person could be sure of his right to keep it. The courts were corrupt. Judges made their living from bribes and excessive fees won from helpless people. Conspiracies and plots were so common that the people did not dare to trust any group or person.

---

[1] Marc Connelly, *Green Pastures*, Holt, Rinehart & Winston, 1958, p.17.

As I watched the congressional hearings on television these past weeks, I was struck by the relevancy of the words with which Hosea opens the case against the nation of Israel:

> Children of Israel, listen to the words of Yahweh, for Yahweh indicts the inhabitants of the country.There is no fidelity, no tenderness,no knowledge of God in the country, only perjury and lies.[2]

Amos had watched these ease-loving people loll in idleness and luxury; Hosea saw those same people hardened and made criminal by the conditions that surrounded them. Bloodshed, highway robbery, murder, and organized vice were visible at every hand. The priests were actually at the head of organized bandit gangs and were instigators of rackets. In such a society, the people had lost their self-reliance; fear and uncertainty gripped them and rendered them helpless. Family life had gone to pieces. Worship of foreign cults had broken down the old standards of morality and faithfulness. The concentration of wealth in the hands of a few had born it's natural fruits in class hatreds, in oppressive measures, in evictions from homes, in desperate deeds of retaliation, and in actual slavery for many who could not cope.

It was during these years of anarchy and bloodshed, of revolt and breakup of the nation, that the prophet Hosea preached in Israel. He was called to deliver God's message to a people with very little concern for spiritual matters. They had not listened to Amos, and they were not disposed to give Hosea heed either.

We don't know a lot about Hosea. He was a native of the Northern Kingdom, he devoutly loved his country and people, and he spent his entire life in an unceasing effort to call them back to God. He tells us about this in a dramatic personal story that lays bare all that happened in his own life.

Hosea was married to a beautiful young woman. He had not known her for long before their marriage, but he knew of rumors that

---

[2] *Hosea* 4:1.

she was a rather frivolous woman who had been in and out of love several times. He thought, however, that even if that were true, she was now more mature, and assumed that he could meet all her needs.

Things apparently went well for the young couple for several years, though there were some difficult moments. Hosea recognized their first child as his own, but he could not claim their second child or their third. Several times his wife threatened to move out and leave him, but Hosea genuinely and idealistically loved her and did everything within his power to please her. However, Gomar was unwilling or incapable of returning his love, and she eventually left him to become involved in shallow, promiscuous relations with others.

Hosea was beside himself with suffering, not only because he loved her but because he recognized her need. He knew she could not find true happiness in her erratic wanderings or in her series of fleeting thrills that turned sour with the morning dawn. So he continued to love her, hoping desperately that she would come back to him. But she did not.

As time went on, one of her lovers tired of Gomar and sold her into slavery. Hosea went out to seek her, and he found her. He went to her owner and bought her for fifteen pieces of silver and a bushel and a half of wheat. Then he brought her back to his heart and home, where she found what she could never find in her wanderings. She found love tender, firm, real, and secure, the kind of love that could transform her and give meaning and purpose to a life that once had been empty and fruitless.

This is a story of a deathless kind of love. Even around the ruins of her life, the wishes of Hosea's heart were still entwined. Out of this experience, perhaps in the very midst of it, Hosea discovered and articulated the concept of the love of God. For he turned the whole heartbreaking experience into an illustration of what was happening between the nation and Yahweh.

Like Gomar, Israel was running out and saying, "I'm going to court my lovers who give me my bread and water, my wool, my flax, my oil, and my drink." Israel would not acknowledge that Yahweh was the one who was so freely giving her the corn, the wine and the oil. Yahweh wanted Israel to understand that these Canaanite lovers were utterly helpless to give her the gifts for which she followed them.

Then follows a beautiful picture of the inextinguishable love of God seeking to hold his willful bride. Hosea has Yahweh say,

> See, now, I will be the one who attracts her, and
> brings her into a desert place, and speaks gently
> to her inmost heart. From there I will give her
> vineyards, and turn the valley of Bitterness into
> a pass which is bright with promise. And there
> she will respond as she did in the days of her
> youth, as she did at the time when she came
> out of the land of Egypt. [3]

This is Yahweh, the Creator of the whole world, speaking in terms of memories of the old honeymoon days. Yahweh wanted them renewed and believed that he could win Israel again to himself. So Yahweh sings as in the good old days. He promises that the ugly past will be forgotten, that the new marriage will be an eternal affair. And just as Hosea goes out and buys Gomar back, so will Yahweh buy back wayward Israel and restore her.

What a fantastic thought this is. This mighty God creates men and women out of love, and makes them free creatures that they may receive love and respond in love to the gift of life and joy. This mighty God holds them and cares for them through the experience of the Exodus, through the Red Sea and the Wilderness, and gives them the land. But these blessed people then turn from their loving creator God to pursue foolish pleasures and temporal treasures; they rebel against their creator, their lover, to go whoring after the delights of this world, after lesser gods, idols and images.

But the eternal love of this creator God never ceases even in the midst of all this. Yahweh allows them to discover for themselves the emptiness of their lives, the suffering they bring upon themselves through their unfaithfulness and rebellion. Yahweh knew well that even in their despair they could not find their way back to him. And so, with loving

---

[3] *Hosea* 2:14-15.

mercy, Yahweh pursued them in their suffering, hurting, and agonizing, seeking to draw them back into his forgiving heart and to restore them to a loving relationship.

As frivolous and foolish as his wayward creatures are at times, God pours out his affection upon them and tenderly speaks to them about a coming day when they shall fully know and experience his infinite love, when all their conflicts will be dissolved, their hurts healed, their sorrows washed away, and the deepest longing of their hearts met and satisfied. On that great day they shall know without doubt that Yahweh is their God and they are Yahweh's children. And so this mighty God pursues them with loving mercy, and shares their sufferings and sorrows.

Even in our day, when the love of God is even further revealed through the life of Jesus, Yahweh's children break out of his circle of tender concern and love to play the harlot with creatures and things, philosophies and ideologies, false religions and cults. These things promise security, ecstacy, riches, and self-satisfaction, but they always fail to deliver true joy because they are incapable of meeting the real eternal needs of God's creatures.

But Yahweh does not give up. As we saw in the play *Green Pastures*, the Lord will not admit he's licked. So, even while we call judgement down upon ourselves, God is always ready to forgive. When we stumble into the pits that await us, God is always waiting and ready to draw us back. The greatest message of both Old and New Testament is that God is love. God stands ready to forgive our infidelities and heal our faithlessness, for that is the problem with true love: it never lets go. And we're back to our scripture:

> How profoundly I love my children whom I
> have created and to whom I have imparted my
> spirit! I continue to reveal to them My com-
> passion; I help to bear their burdens and ac-
> company them through the adversities that
> afflict them; I heal many of their sicknesses
> and demonstrate My loving concern in the midst
> of their deep sorrows and excruciating suffer-
> ings; I hold out to them my salvation and invite

them to partake of My saving and redeeming grace.

When they refuse to follow me, I will follow them even into the dark, cold caves of nothingness, into the pits of despair, seeking always to draw them back to my redeeming love, to restore them to My will for them.[4]

For God is love. . . .

a love that gives and expects no return . . .

a love that lives for others . . .

*   *   *   *   *

The story of Hosea is found in the book by that name in the Bible.

---

[4] A paraphrase of *Hosea* 11 from *Prophets Now* by Leslie F. Brandt, Concordia Publishing House, St. Louis, p. 78-79.

Chapter Fifteen

A MAN WITH A
WHALE OF A PROBLEM

It is a terrible tragedy that we have misused Jonah for so long; ask the average person what they think of when you say "Jonah" and they will say "whale." Yet only three verses in the whole book of Jonah say anything about the incident with the whale, and it is a pity that the value and beauty of this book has been obscured by a fish story which has been swallowed whole by so many people. For example, the story has given rise to controversy over how it would be possible for a fish to swallow a man; just so we can get on with the story, the answer is that it is no particular problem since Jonah was one of the *minor* prophets!

This is one of the most delightful stories in the Old Testament; it was written by a genius at storytelling, a master of language with a touch of humor and a touch of pathos. The "book" of Jonah is actually a missionary tract; it was no more intended to be read as straight history than was the parable of the Good Samaritan or that of the Wise and Foolish Virgins. The author of this magnificent document would turn over in the grave at the thought of taking the words literally.

The writer of Jonah was on fire with a great message; he would teach his people a great truth, that "the love of God is broader than the measure of man's mind," as a constant rebuke to our pretensions, our narrow judgments, and our divisions. He sets the meanness and foolishness of men and women against the background of the greatness, and goodness, and love of Yahweh. Against the background of the great dream of the universal human caring, he places this present world torn asunder by antagonisms. But, his problem was how best to drive home the lesson. How could he put it so that people would easily grasp the message? His solution was to tell his own story of an encounter with God made especially vivid for the word picture.

Jonah had been a narrow, tight man, a first class nationalist who hated all foreigners. But the author tells of Jonah's call to go and warn and give mercy to, of all places in the world, Nineveh, the capital of the dread Assyrian Empire, the most hated and feared of Israel's oppressors. Then, in contrast to his first point of view, he shows a portrait of the love and mercy of Yahweh. This is like Yahweh coming to William Buckley and telling him that God loves the Soviets and that he, William Buckley had to go and tell them that, so that they might be saved.

And so the missionary tract begins:

> The word of Yahweh was addressed to Jonah son of Amittai: "Up!" he said, "Go to Nineveh, the great city, and inform them that their wickedness has become known to me." Jonah decided to run away from Yahweh, and to go to Tarshish. [1]

Jonah was living about four miles north of Nazareth. He was a proud, self-centered citizen of Israel. For centuries the Israelites had constantly been invaded by Assyrians, Egyptians, Moabites and others; at the moment they had found some peace form all this and were enjoying it. Then all of a sudden, Jonah was chosen for a mission. Yahweh said to Jonah, "Go to Nineveh!" And Jonah says, "I'll go to Tarshish." Yahweh tells him to go to Nineveh, and Jonah goes out telling his friends that he feels called to go to Tarshish. There were no Presbyterians in Nineveh, you see, but there were in Tarshish. Besides it's cold in Nineveh, and it's sunny and warm in Tarshish. More than that, in Nineveh they were not of Jonah's cultural background as they were in Tarshish. And look, Yahweh, it costs less money to take the ship for Tarshish. Yes, Jonah felt called to go preach in Tarshish.

So Jonah went right down to the docks and took the first ship to Tarshish. See how this would capture the interest and sympathy of people to whom the very thought of salvation for the gentiles was abhorrent? Jonah was doing just what they would have done.

---

[1] *Jonah* 1:1-3.

But all did not go well. Yahweh is still calling Jonah to go to Nineveh, and Jonah pictures this struggle in his mind as a great storm on board a ship. And quite a storm it is. The superstitious crew cast lots to see who on board is responsible, and the lot falls on poor Jonah. But the ship's crew were not a lynching party; first they threw overboard all the cotton and sandalwood they were carrying (that was the cheapest cargo), to see if that would balance the ship and save it. When that does not work, the brass vases and cooking pots go overboard. but still the storm rages and they are about to sink. Then, Jonah nobly offers to sacrifice his own life that the others in the boat might be saved.

Readers of this missionary tract would perhaps not notice the inconsistency of Jonah being willing to give his life to save gentile sailors, but not being able to bear the thought that Yahweh would save the gentiles in Nineveh. Even the most vengeful person might commend Jonah for his self-sacrifice in this instance, for their faith had taught them to be considerate of others. Jonah could have mercy on the gentiles in this one particular instance, but Yahweh must not have mercy on them. No, Yahweh must have only wrath for the gentiles.

Thus, this prophet exposes in his own person the absurdity of an attitude which prevailed among many of his fellow citizens. It is as though he were drawing a caricature of them and holding it up so that they might recognize themselves. It's OK to be nice to an individual Russian who comes here to visit, but be ready to nuke the whole nation at a moments notice.

But, Jonah now finds himself up against it. Note that this turning point in his life comes at the very depths of his pursuit of disobedience. Since first he said "no" to Yahweh, he had gone *down* to Joppa, *down* into a ship, *down* into the hold, and at last *down* into the watery depths. His final descent into the ocean depths would have been his last had he not had a change of heart on deck, but not until he was all the way down, finally stripped of his own sense of self-sufficiency, was deliverance possible.

In his telling of his encounter with Yahweh, he portrays it as being in the belly of a fish. The Hebrew is very vivid here, it says: "And Jonah cried out of his 'tight spot.'" Hasn't that been the experience of many of us: In a tight spot, knowing what we ought to do, but unwilling to sacrifice personal pride and prejudice?

There is an old story of a man who didn't believe in giving to foreign mission. One day as the offering plate was being passed to take up a special mission offering, the usher put it before him. He put noting in but said, "I don't believe in foreign missions." The usher pushed the plate back to him and said, "Then take some out, it's for the heathen."

Jonah really wrestles with himself now. He is caught in his own little corner, in his own tight spot, and Yahweh will not let him go. It's like the experience Francis Thompson describes in *Hound of Heaven*:

> I fled Him, down the nights and down the days;
> I fled Him, down the arches of the years;
> I fled him, down the labyrinthine ways
> Of my own mind; and in the midst of tears
> I hid from Him, and under running laughter.
> Up vistaed hopes I sped;
> And shot, precipitated,
> A down Titanic glooms of chasmed fears,
> From those strong Feet that followed, followed
>   after.
> But with unhurrying chase,
> And unperturbed pace,
> Deliberate speed, majestic instancy
> They beat--and a Voice beat
> More instant than the Feet--
> 'All things betray thee, who betrayest Me.'[2]

You see, even after we have turned our backs on Yahweh, even after we purchase tickets for Tarshish when Yahweh wants us to go to Nineveh, Yahweh is still with us, still by our side; we are not alone.

Yahweh spoke to the fish which then vomited Jonah onto the shore, and the stage is set for the final act of the story.

---

[2] Francis Thompson, "Hound of Heaven," *Modern British Poetry* (Louis Untermeyer, editor), 1955, Harcourt Brace & Co., p. 297.

Here is Jonah's second chance, with the same God, the same word, the same purpose. Chapter 3 begins:

> The word of Yahweh was addressed a second
> time to Jonah: "Up!" he said, "Go to Nineveh,
> the great city, and preach to them as I told you
> to."

Jonah now turns and goes God's way. After a real encounter with Yahweh, how can a person do anything less? Going against God's will is suicide; Jonah knew that! So he arrives at the great city of Nineveh, with the same word and the same purpose from the same God. Unfortunately, it is also the same Jonah, by and large. He is still a first-class nationalist, still exalting his own country, his own people, and his own God. He will give reluctant obedience but there is no mercy in his heart.

Nineveh had 120,000 inhabitants at that time, with a wall eighty feet high and wide enough for three chariots to race abreast on the top. The reluctant missionary marched into the city and stood in the center of the market place and there prepared to give his first sermon. At least he could take relish in that, for Jonah liked the text of his sermon. He said: "Only forty days more and Nineveh is going to be destroyed." No hope, just judgment! Then he took himself over to the top of a little hill outside the city and waited for the great event. Maybe this will not be such a bad task after all, he must have thought, for these people surely will not heed my word or Yahweh's.

But then something happened; beginning with the King himself and extending all the way down to the lowest servant, the people repented and believed in Yahweh! Something happened in that city that we certainly do not expect to happen in Chicago. They were converted.

This was the last straw for Jonah. The poor man just broke down and cried, and his words sound ridiculous:

> See, I knew it would happen. I knew what kind
> of a God you are Yahweh. That's why I didn't
> want to come here. I knew that you are a

> gracious God and merciful, slow to anger and
> abounding in steadfast love.[3]

He knew God would save the enemy, but he didn't want them saved! He
was scared to death that it would work, and it did.

Jonah's narrow ideology was in conflict with Yahweh's love.
Jonah's blinkers gave him a too-narrow view. He was jealous; his
jealousy evoked a garbled view of Yahweh, and it shows that he never
understood the God of love in the first place.

And now comes the final decisive touch in this masterful piece of
writing. Jonah has been spared at this point, but his therapy must still be
completed.

Jonah is sitting outside the city sulking and pouting like a child.
It's very hot, and all of a sudden Yahweh has a gourd plant grow up right
behind Jonah to give him luscious shade. The next night, Yahweh has
a worm come and kill the plant, and the following day, when the sun
came up, it got hot, and still hotter. To add to his discomfort, a wind
from the desert brought in an eastern sirocco with such intense heat and
dust that even indoor living became intolerable, and here is Jonah sitting
outside with no protection.

And Jonah complains bitterly about the loss of "his" gourd plant.
"What did that plant do to you, Lord?" he asked. And God says to
Jonah,

> You are upset about the plant which cost you no
> labor, which you did not make grow, which
> sprouted in a night and has perished in a night.
> And am I not to feel sorry for Nineveh, the
> great city, in which there are more than a
> hundred and twenty thousand people, to say
> nothing of all the animals? [4]

---

[3] *Jonah* 4:1-2.

[4] *Jonah* 4:10-11.

Jonah was profoundly disappointed that God, creator of all humankind, did not wipe out thousands of his fellow humans. He was equally disappointed that God, creator of all plants and animals, would allow a weevil to waste a single plant. The death of the plant was a personal inconvenience to him, whereas the death of multitudes was of no immediate concern!

Someone once said that the Book of Jonah is an unfinished symphony, and it does tend to leave you that way. It ends with a last question that Yahweh puts to Jonah, and Jonah doesn't answer. It is naturally disappointing for us not to know whether Jonah finally understood; did he reply in humility and adoration, or did he turn his back another time? But, in reality, Jonah can not reply; the question is the question of the life and death of the world, not just the salvation of Jonah. He could not answer the question because the question is put to each of us. It becomes our eternal question. It is the question of responsibility, and it is a question about your God.

First, how big is your God? You can get away from a little God in a little boat on a little sea, but you cannot get away from Yahweh.

Then, is your God the creator of all the universe, the God of all the nations (as the Old Testament would phrase it), or is your God an American God? How much of a religious isolationist are you? How deep an interest has the God in whom you believe in those areas of the world which are hostile to the things you hold dear as an American?

If Yahweh has a controversy with his people today, it is because we are so selfish, because our main preoccupation is with ourselves, because our reaction to every new proposal is "How will this affect me, my wealth, my position, my prestige, my future?"

If Yahweh has a controversy with his people today, it is because there has been too little concern for our brothers and sisters, too little recognition that their fate is bound up with ours in this tiny spaceship called Earth, too much forgetting that we are, in the words of Paul, "members one of another."

If Yahweh has a controversy with his people today, it is because there has been too little recognition of our common humanity and our common destiny with all the people of the earth, whether of Taiwan and Afghanistan, of Nicaragua and Rumania, of South Africa and Sudan; it is because we make too convenient an assumption that we are not our brother's keeper.

A Jonah lurks in every Christian heart, whispering an insidious message of smug prejudice, empty traditionalism, and exclusive solidarity. We grasp the message of this story only when we eleminate the Jonah within us. As the great fish coughed Jonah up onto the beach, so too must we reject from within us the Jonah of prejudice and shame.

*   *   *   *   *

The story of Jonah is found in the book by that name in the Old Testament.

Chapter Sixteen

OH SUSANNA!

This "Bible story you never heard before" comes from a part of the Bible called the Apocrypha. The term "apocrypha" is a Greek word meaning "hidden things." It originally was applied to writings that were regarded as so important and precious that they had to be hidden from the general public and reserved for initiates or an inner circle of believers. The term later came to be applied to writings that were hidden not because they were too good, but because they were thought to be secondary, questionable, or heretical.

For a time, the books of the Apocrypha were included in the Jewish canon and were used as part of their sacred writings. But, after the fall of Jerusalem in A.D. 70, they were rejected by Jewish scholars. The story of Susanna is rough on "elders," as you will see, and since the "elders" were the ones doing the choosing, it is perhaps no surprise that Susanna didn't make it.

The books of the Apocrypha were kept on in the collected writings of the early Christians. For instance, Augustine put these books on a par with the rest of the Old Testament and quoted them frequently. During the Reformation, when great emphasis was placed on the supremacy and purity of the Bible there was an effort to reject the Apocrypha; this was at least partly because Catholic scholars used texts from the Apocrypha against the arguments of the reformers. This ecclesiastical-political use of the books was one of the major reasons that we Protestants have, for centuries, not studied them.

Fortunately this question is no longer hotly argued, and we have come to see that these books shed a lot of historical light on New Testament times. For instance, the book called *I Maccabees* bridges the gap of history just before the birth of Jesus. But enough of this, and on with our story.

The story of Susanna is considered the gem of the apocrypha. It is one of the best short stories in world literature, and it is based on the familiar theme of the triumph of virtue over villainy, including a narrow escape from death by an innocent victim. It is among the earliest detective stories, and Dorothy Sayers included it at the very beginning of her anthology of mysteries entitled *Omnibus of Crime,* published in 1929, as a model of the genre.

The story concerns Daniel (remember him in the lion's den?), and is seen as an addition to the *Book of Daniel* in the Old Testament. It is a lesson about purity and trust in God, and it proclaims the moral that God does not desert the innocent who trust and pray. It begins:

> There once lived in Babylon a man named Joakim. He married Susanna daughter of Hilkiah, a very beautiful and devout woman. Her parents, religious people, had brought up their daughter according to the law of Moses. Joakim was very rich and his house had a fine garden adjoining it, which was a regular meeting-place for the Jews, because he was the man of greatest distinction among them. [1]

The story is set in Babylon, a city that was at that time reported to be the most beautiful in the world, and containing the great hanging gardens of Nebuchadnezzar, one of the seven wonders of the ancient world. In this very beautiful city, a very beautiful young woman by the name of Susanna lived with her husband Joakim. Joakim was wealthy and was held in great respect by the people. He was one of the leaders of the Jewish community, perhaps *the* leader, and his prestige was matched by his wife's beauty and by her devotion to him and to Yahweh. We are told early in the story that her parents saw that she was instruct-

---

[1] *Daniel and Susanna* 1-4.

ed in the law of Moses; it must have been a good education, for it took well.

In those days, the grounds around a wealthy persons's home were often open in the morning for other members of the community to do business. Law business was especially likely to be handled in this way. The Jewish elders and judges would come and hold court in Joakim's estate. After they had brought their suits of law, everyone would gradually depart around noon.

At mid-day, Susanna would take a walk in her garden; she would enter as the people were leaving, so they could see her and pass the time of day with her. But there were two elders who watched her every day in a more than casual way. Unmindful of Yahweh's command, they became inflamed with passion for her. Fully conscious of the impropriety of their desires and the law that prohibited such a thing, they tried to conceal their feelings.

One day, at about the noon hour, it happened that these two elders said good-bye to one another and both made for the garden gate as if to leave. Both then sneaked back into the garden, unobserved, to hide and watch Susanna even longer than normal. Low and behold, they ended up in the same hiding spot! They were astounded and embarrassed to see one another, and they obviously had to confess to each other their lustful desires. Thereafter these two pulled the same trick almost daily, making a big show of leaving for mid-day meals, but really lingering in the garden and watching Susanna from the bushes.

One very hot day, while these two were hidden in the garden, Susanna decided to take a bath in the pool. No one was about, except, of course, the two elders spying from their hiding place. Susanna said to her maidservants, "Bring me some oil and balsam and shut the garden door while I bathe." They did as they were told, shut the garden door, and went back into the house, leaving Susanna alone.

No sooner had the maids disappeared than the two elders ran to Susanna and said, "Look, the garden door is shut and no one can see us. We want to have you, so give in and let us." These two practicing lawyers had thought out a few things in advance; they went on to say, "If you refuse us, we will both give evidence that we saw a young man with you and that is why you sent your maids away."

Susanna was beside herself. "I am trapped, whatever I do," she groaned. "If I do agree, the penalty for such a sin against Yahweh is death, if I resist I will be at your mercy." But then she took a step of faith and said, "but I prefer to fall innocent into your power than to sin in the eyes of God." So she let out as loud a scream as she could and set up a huge commotion for all to hear.

The elders began to shout as well. One of them ran and opened the garden door, and they both yelled at the top of their lungs for the family to come to the garden and see what evil had taken place. The whole household came into the garden to see what was happening.

The elders told their concocted story; they said they had found Susanna committing adultery with a young man who had dashed away when they attempted to detain him. "He was too young and strong, we couldn't hold him. But we saw the whole sinful act. He ran out that door in the garden wall." The servants were shocked, for no word of scandal had ever before been breathed about their mistress' virtue. Everyone knew that Susanna was a good woman.

The following day the court was again in session in the garden of Joakim. The judges summoned Susanna before them, and the two elders, filled with vindictiveness, determined that they were going to put her to death for not giving in to them. Susanna came into the garden with her parents and children. The book says:

> Now Susanna was a woman of great beauty.
> She was closely veiled, but those scoundrels
> ordered her to be unveiled so that they might
> feast their eyes on her beauty.[2]

The two elders stood up and publicly repeated their indictment, laying their hands on the head of Susanna in accordance with the code that is written in Leviticus, even though they knew the indictment was

---

[2] *Daniel and Susanna* 31-32.

false. Susanna turned her eyes to heaven, confident in Yahweh. The elders testified:

> As we were walking by ourselves in the garden, this woman arrived with two servants. She shut the garden door, dismissed the servants, and a young man who had been hiding went over to her and they laid down together. We were in a corner of the garden, and when we saw this wickedness we ran up to them. Though we saw them in the act, we could not hold the man; he was too strong for us, and he opened the door and forced his way out. We seized the woman and asked who the young man was, but she would not tell us. That is our evidence. [3]

Susanna protested her innocence and raised her voice in prayer to Yahweh. But, since the accusation was made by such highly respected elders, it was believed to be true, and she was convicted and sentenced to death. She was led away through the streets to be stoned to death.

However, according to the code of the people, when a person was condemned to death for a crime, the sentence was given by the whole community, not just by the judges. In that way, everyone shouldered a piece of the responsibility. This procedure is often misunderstood, for when a person was condemned to death, they were led through the streets to the place of death for a reason. Someone went in advance, calling out that anyone who had evidence to the contrary should come forth, whoever they were, and give that evidence, so that the person, if innocent, would be saved.

So here is the scene. A procession through the streets of the elders and the people, with Susanna in tow. A crier went in front of the

---

[3] *Daniel and Susanna* 36-40.

parade calling out for anyone to step forth and give new evidence if they had it, in order that Susanna might be saved. And sure enough, the procession was dramatically interrupted by a young man named Daniel, who demanded the right to interrogate the witnesses! He cried,

> Are you so stupid, sons of Israel, as to condemn
> a daughter of Israel unheard and without trou-
> bling to find the truth? Go back to the scene
> of the trial, these men have given false evidence
> against her.[4]

The people were delighted, and everyone hurried back to the garden. There the judges said to Daniel, "Come sit with us, and tell us what you mean." But Daniel first insisted that the two elders involved be separated and that they be brought before the court one at a time to be cross-examined.

The first elder was summoned and Daniel boldly said:

> "You old relic of wicked days, your sins have
> now come home which you have committed in
> the past, pronouncing unjust judgement, con-
> demning the innocent, letting the guilty go free.
> Now tell us if you really saw her in this act so
> clearly, tell us under which tree did you see
> them being intimate?" He replied, "Under the
> clove tree." Then Daniel had the other man
> brought in and confronted him with the same
> question. And this one said, "I saw it take place
> under the yew tree over there."[5]

---

[4] *Daniel and Susanna* 48-49.

[5] *Daniel and Susanna* 52-59.

It was clear that the two lied, and one of the neat things that is often missed is the play on words here. The first elder said he saw Susanna and her lover under a clove tree and Daniel says, "You have lied and Yahweh will *cleave* you in two;" to the other, who said he saw them under the yew tree, Daniel said, "Yahweh will *hew* you in two."

The whole assembly shouted and praised Yahweh, but then they turned to the two elders whom Daniel had convicted of giving false evidence. Again following the code prescribed by the law of Moses, they sentenced them to the same punishment they had intended to inflict on Susanna. The two elders were put to death, and the life of an innocent woman was spared that day.

The story of Susanna concludes with these lines: "From that day onward, Daniel's reputation stood high with the people."

St. John Chrysostom, a great early preacher in the church at Constantinople in A.D. 385 said:

> She [Susanna] stood as a lamb between two wolves, she was left alone between these two beasts with no one to help her but God alone. And God looked down from heaven and suffered the dispute to make clear both the chastity of Susanna and the wickedness of the elders so that she might become a glorious example to women of all times.

Less poetically put, the point is that Susanna stood fast in her faith and trust. Nothing shook her. And look at all the pressure on her: a slander against her fidelity to her marriage vow; the fear of death; the condemnation of all the people; the tears of her servants; and the grief of her household.

Some scholars regard this story as a tract of the times, satirizing the current administration of justice. The author was concerned about laxity and abuse in the process of conducting legal matters, and it was an appeal for a more rigid examination of witnesses in cases where collusion might be suspected. It is also an appeal to curb perjury, demanding infliction of the same punishment on a perjurer as his victim would have suffered had the deceit not been detected.

And, it is a model to women everywhere, who, in increasing numbers are courageously and at great personal cost, are protesting the violence done them in sexual assault. It is a warning, too, to law enforcement officers, to attorneys, and to judges and juries who fail to see how serious a matter this is with the Susannas of our day. So protest loud and clear, Susanna, and may Yahweh raise up for us more Daniels!

*   *   *   *   *

This story is found in the book *Susanna and Daniel* in the Bible.